The Children of the Poor

Penny Kay Hoeflinger

With Sylvia Dorham

Coffeehouse Farm
P.O. Box 669
Gerrardstown, WV 25420

Children of the Poor

My sickness, Child, I leave to you
There isn't any cure.
My parents passed it down to me,
We're Children of the Poor.

There's no one to defend us here,
Want is our daily bread.
Of love or opportunity
The crumbs alone we're fed.

The little that we call our own
They come and take away,
With force and lies and laws which are
Beyond our strength to stay.

In horror and disappointment,
In anger, fear, and shame,
We use what we can find at hand
To try and dull the pain

Oh, hide me away, someplace where
My shame cannot be seen
I'm less, not wanted, tossed aside
As if I'd never been.

At eternal disadvantage,
Inclined to evil's lure
The trafficked, angry masses, we,
The Children of the Poor

- Sylvia Dorham

The ransom of a man's life is his wealth, but a poor man has no means of redemption.
Proverbs 13:8

Dear Reader,

Our memories are confused in the drug and alcohol world. There are months of our lives that are just gone – we couldn't tell you what happened, where we were, what we did. Then there are blackouts. Those are really scary. We drive cars, cook meals, even operate on people – and have no mental connection to what we're doing. It's scary.

This is a memoir. It's what I remember from many years of darkness. Most parts are accurate, but in some places, the facts may be fuzzy. Forgive me, please, for misremembered details and instead take from these pages the lessons I have learned putting all these pieces back together.

Your Friend,

Penny Kay

If you have been through a lot, you have a choice. You can feel like the world owes you, or you can be compassionate and live a humble life. I chose the latter.

*

My earliest memory is of sleeping on the back of the big white horse.

I am lying there, staring up into the wide, blue Wyoming sky, speaking to my guardian angels.

The horse is enormous, and I can't be more than two, maybe three years old, but he tolerates me climbing up his tail onto his back and is careful to keep me from falling off.

There are other memories, too. Further back.

In one, I am present in a council meeting before my birth. We are gathered somewhere out there in the universe, and I am not in my body. In this council meeting, I am the essence of a being. A soul, perhaps. Other beings are there with me. You can tell the difference between them because some of them are more powerful than others. The powerful ones are talking to me about the course of study I have put together for myself to learn. I don't want to come to earth to learn the lessons, though. I can see the earth from the council chambers, and the craziness and slaughter is clearly visible. I want to write the lessons down, but they want me to actually go to Earth to teach compassion. I already know compassion, not in an academic sense, but with this essence of knowing.

Suddenly, I am in my mother's stomach. The next thing I can remember for certain are those cherry chocolates my mother loves so much. My mother is so mad at Daddy. She is lying across her bed, yelling and calling him every name in the book, stuffing her mouth with chocolates.

Years later, I ask my mom, "Why were you so mad at Daddy?"

"Which time?" my mother quips.

"The time you were lying on the bed eating cherry chocolates." I recount the names she had called him.

"How do you know that?" she asks, peering at me closely.

"Because I saw you," I reply.

"How could you have seen me, Penny Kay? I was six months pregnant with you at the time."

I do not want to stay here. But here I am.

My next awareness is in the hospital. I have decided I want out of this body, but my mother does not want me to be born before Mothers' Day. She walks with her legs tight together and sits on the edge of the bed to keep me from coming down, but I come the day before Mother's Day 1947, in Thermopolis, Wyoming.

The spirit beings, the angels, are still with me. I can see them. The veil that usually separates the physical world from the spiritual, the curtain that keeps us from seeing across the Divide, is still open. I am filled with a pure knowledge of God. God is God. I am pure of heart, and I can tell when someone's intentions are not pure.

I begin my life without seeing a car. In fact, I don't lay eyes on one until I am six years of age because Daddy always uses the horses and a buck wagon. We are too poor to buy a car.

My mother tells me frequently that I am not normal.

At six months, I scream all night, my body covered in bumps.

At nine months, I suddenly decide I am done crawling and just start walking, giving myself access to the outside world.

At two, my dad comes to the barn where he keeps a wild mustang and finds me standing between its quivering hind legs, pulling its tail and petting him. My dad stands in the doorway and tries to coax me out in a calm voice. He knows the "horey" will trample me to death if he tries to go in and get me. When I finally come to my dad, he jerks me out, and *wham*! I cannot sit down for the rest of the day.

One day, my dad is on the way to town in the buck

wagon for supplies. He snaps the whip, but the horses don't move. He tries again and still they don't move. Finally, he gets down to check. There I am, under the bellies of the horses, petting them. From that moment, I have to stay in the house when Dad drives the buck wagon away.

One day, as we prepare to leave Lost Springs and move to Thermopolis so I can go to school, my angels tell me goodbye. They say my life is going to be rough, but they will be there with me. Always.

Our life is one of poverty and perseverance, of trouble and turmoil, but we survive. We always survive.

MY GENEALOGY

Turmoil is not new to my family. My great-grandad on my father's side, Milton Hammond, went to Rawlins penitentiary for killing a man. Years after he died, when my great-grandmother was on her deathbed, she said he had covered for her so she didn't have to go to prison. She was the one who had killed her first husband who beat her.

My story is as turbulent as the land in which I was raised. My ancestors are the people who fought, who tried to do what is right, who fell into vice. I am a child of my people, and I carry their pain. Our pain.

Our story, my story repeats the same themes of sex, religion, suicide, occult, Mormonism, domestic violence, drugs, alcohol, and indomitable spirit. Themes of incomprehensible endurance and great faith.

My father's family were Newells, crusader people from Ireland. The seven Newell brothers crossed the Atlantic and settled in Virginia, West Virginia, and Ohio. Unlike most settlers, the Newells were compassionate to the Native American, helping them at every opportunity.

THE MURDER OF MY GREAT-GRANDMOTHER

On my father's side, my great-grandmother was a full-blooded Cherokee Indian. We don't know her name, in fact, no one talks about her because she and my great-grandfather were having an affair. My great-grandfather, Gus Newell, was married to Elsie Ayles, a descendent of Revolutionary War General Benedict Arnold. With her, he had three children. What my family never spoke about was the identity of the mother of Gus' illegitimate children, Clarence and Nellie. It was easy to guess, though, when Nellie's features and unusual woodcarving skills bore witness to her Native American heritage.

Great-grandpa Gus, who ran a freight line, was easy going and friendly. He was a champion cowboy, a crack shot, and a fearless protector of the underdog. In spite of his popularity, an affair with a Cherokee woman was socially unacceptable in late-19th Century Wyoming.

The West was still wild when my great-grandpa ran his freight line from Tongue River to Bridger, Montana in the 1880s and 90s. At that time, an argument between the big cattlemen and those with smaller holdings erupted into a full-scale fight called The Johnson Cattle War (1889-1893).

Today, cattle and sheep share the pastures, but back then, sheep were despised by the big cattlemen. They didn't realize that the cattle rip out the grass that irrigates and holds the soil in place, but sheep just mow it. My great-grandpa stood up for the rights of the small cattlemen and the sheepherders against the big ranch owners who didn't want any competition. Before long, Gus and his brother were on the cattlemen's wanted list.

I have a theory about why my great-grandmother was killed. She was the Indian mistress of the Cattlemen's enemy, a tool they could use to blackmail him. Maybe they thought the way to make him capitulate was to murder her in front of him and their children.

He didn't capitulate.

10

My great-grandpa was surely forced to watch what they did to my great-grandmother, but he and the children escaped the murderers. When he showed up at Laramie Peak, one hundred and fifty miles away from his home, though, he didn't have Clarence or Nellie with him. What I don't understand is how he was able to get the kids to the cave where they hid after the murder. Maybe the kids knew where to run and find shelter.

My Aunt Katie rode out on horseback from Laramie Peak to find the children. She was a white woman and was able to ride the whole way without being stopped by the rival factions of the Cattle War. When she arrived at the cave, she found the children eating raw rabbit. They were starving and wild, small wonder after seeing their mother murdered. Aunt Kate carried them all the way back to Laramie Peak, where they were separated and sent to live with relatives.

I was thirteen-years-old and living with my parents in Glendo, Wyoming, when my great-uncle Clarence came from Coos Bay, Oregon, to visit. He told me that he and my grandmother had gone to rebury their mother. Great-uncle Clarence and Grandma knew just where to go to get their mother's body, although they never told me the location.

I feel a strong drive to know more about my murdered great-grandmother. I can feel her pushing me hard to find out more.

My cousin, Audrey, and I were doing genealogy research in the Douglas, Wyoming, library when I actually heard her voice. That same day I went to look for her grave in Gilette, where she lived but the voice said, "I'm not here." From there, we went to Sheridan, where she worked with Gus on his freight line. There, we found the marriage certificate of my great-grandpa Gus to his wife, Elsie Ayles. From there, Cousin Audrey and I went to Tongue River, the terminus of the freight line where Clarence and Nellie were born. In a small trading post there we found a bell that I recognized as a part of one of her ceremonial dresses. I began to understand, but the voice said, "Come on! I'm not here! Follow me!"

"What will we do now?" Audrey wondered.

"I can't stop now," I said. And so we drove all the way to Bridger, Montana, the opposite end of the freight line. By the time we got there, it was too dark to go to the graveyard, so we got a hotel room.

In the morning, I could feel my great-grandmother. We went to the cemetery and I felt overwhelmed. It was filled with hundreds of graves. Suddenly, I heard the voice again, "You're in the wrong cemetery."

We went back downtown and asked if there were other cemeteries in town, and they directed us to a graveyard on a little knoll in a cow pasture. I looked around for any bulls before I went in! The voice said, "Come! Come!" and I followed it right to my great-grandmother's grave.

"I can't believe it!" Audrey yelled. "We had the spelling wrong!" That was the reason we didn't find her grave before. There it was at the bottom of Pryor's Mountain in Bridger, Montana.

She won't let go of me. My great-grandmother says to me, "You must tell the story."

"What story?" I ask her. "I don't even know how you died, or who killed you." Maybe I'll find out some day, but this is an example of my family history. I'm from strong stock. Warrior stock. My people stood up for the defenseless and paid a heavy price along the way.

A fighting spirit is not all that came down through my family. We have diaries as far back as the 1850s containing evidence that alcoholism is also strong in our genes.

DAD'S LITTLE MAN

When I was five, my dad and I sat together in the Shoshone Bar in Shoshone, Wyoming, and did whisky shots. He wanted me to do this because I was his "Little Man," his firstborn.

We lived on the ranch during those years, and Dad was completely emotionless. If you wanted to hang with him, you had to be strong. I spent a lot of time and energy proving my strength, making him proud of me.

I would go with him to feed cattle and build fence. When the sun set, you had to go outside and shut the gate so the Hereford bulls wouldn't come up and sleep on the porch of the house. It could crash into pieces under their ponderous weight. So, at night I would go with a flashlight and shut the gate. I would say, "I can do that," and I would, even though I was just a little girl and those bulls were huge. The flashlight would hit their eyes and terrify me. I would run as fast as I could back to the house, then stop, catch my breath and walk in calmly.

"Was you scared?" my Dad would ask.

"Nope," I said, every time.

He knew better, but his philosophy was that the only thing to fear is fear itself. He instilled in me that fear is an illusion and, therefore, a person can get through anything. He ingrained me with that.

SIBLINGS

My brother, Darr Dwayne, was born in 1949, and with his birth, everything changed. When my brother started to walk, he got the "Little Man" position. It hurt to be replaced like that. I felt rejected, abandoned, and worthless. Not long after, I was raped and my life just started crumbling. Totally crumbling.

In 1953, four years after my brother was born, my little sister, Patricia, came along.

Neither of them went through the suffering that I did. I left home when I was sixteen, so I didn't know my sister very well until just a few years ago. I had nothing to do with my brother, because my dad just forgot about me when he arrived.

13

Daddy had my brother, Mom had my sister, and I was just left to my own devices. Even today, life gets really hard because I always have to be the strong one, the one who takes care of herself. God is there with me, but I am never allowed to be weak. Even in the moments when I do break down, I always have to be the one taking care of the situation. There's no one else to do it for me. That reality started early, and it molded the person I became.

CRUELTY

Fixed in my mind is a moment when a mother cat from the ranch found its way inside our house and had kittens in a box with some of my brother's baby clothes in it. My dad was furious at the birth mess all over the clothes. The next day, the tomcat, the father of the kittens came around. My dad had had enough of cats. He grabbed a .22 and shot the tom in the mouth. His aim was off, and the tom ran away with half of his cheek torn off. My dad cussed and cussed, then grabbed a gunnysack and threw the kittens inside. He took me with him to the river and I watched as he threw the sack into the water. For days, the mama cat cried and cried. Then she disappeared, leaving me with a new understanding of cruelty. In retrospect, I can see this and other events as evidence of the pain my dad was experiencing inside himself. Hurting people hurt others.

More than once he laid into me about my compassion for animals.

"We'd starve if we had to rely on you!" he yelled after a deer got away because I hesitated to pull the trigger. Another time I couldn't break the neck of a cottontail rabbit that screamed in terror. He never took me hunting again. The message came through perfectly. If you didn't conform to his standards, my dad would throw you away.

14

Dad ruled our family with an unrelenting glare. My mom called him "Snake Eyes" for the way he could root you to the ground with his stare.

He had a vicious way of teasing you that left you in despair. He mocked and undermined my teachers until my academic accomplishments and love of school died quietly.

Later, when he died, our family heaved a collective sigh of release. The dictator was gone! We were free! My mom went out and bought the lacy curtains she had always wanted, but had been forbidden to buy. We had spaghetti for dinner, a dish never allowed by my strictly meat-and-potatoes dad. It was a side of him the world never saw, this heavy-fistedness.

My dad was a soldier in the Korean War. Several times he earned his sergeant stripes and then did something to have them stripped. Still, he earned a medal for bravery, along with a tiny pair of gold boxing gloves he earned for boxing. Twice during the war he was shot. One went into his chest and was stopped by a wad of money he carried in his breast pocket. The second time he took a bullet in the rear end, which was stopped by his billfold. Money served him well in Korea!

He came home with PTSD, although there was no name for it at that time. We knew always to call his name from across the room if we needed to wake him. If you touched him or shook him awake he'd come up swinging. Dad did a lot of talking with his fists.

DEATH OF INNOCENCE

My dad, like Hammond men for generations, was a cowboy, and was hired to run the ranch in Lost Spring, Wyoming, where we lived. Dad left ranching for construction because he wasn't making enough money to support our family.

Besides, my mom was pregnant again and didn't want to be isolated out on the ranch. Also, I had to go to school, and since there were no buses, we moved to town.

When I was six years old and in first grade at the town elementary school, a fourteen-year-old boy raped me on the playground. He said he put a watermelon seed in my belly. I told my Mother, who grabbed a .22 and went down the street to kill him.

My dad stopped her.

We went to court and stood before the judge in Thermopolis. The judge told me I was a very bad little girl for tempting the boy. His family had money. His parents were very big in the community, donating money to all kinds of organizations. Way back then, there was no one to advocate for the poor like there would be today. This may be the root of an underlying fear I have that if I have money I will not have a compassionate heart.

I think my dad would have liked to kill that boy, too, but he had his hands full trying to deal with my mother.

After age six, I really didn't have any more childhood. There was no more innocence.

GRANDMOTHER

As a small child, my grandmother, Nellie Hammond, the daughter Gus Newell's murdered mistress, initiated me with an Indian rite of passage that she and countless other children raised by Native American parents had experienced.

One night, after digging out a shallow, flat-bottomed pit on the rolling hills, she handed me a blanket and said it was time for me to go alone into the wilderness and stay there until the rocks spoke to me.

At first, I felt fear, but my father had told me so often that the only thing to fear was fear itself, that it wasn't long before I felt calm under the brilliant stars. I wrapped the blanket

16

around me, completely unaware of my grandmother, seated in the shadows not a hundred feet away. During that long, star-lit night, I learned to hear the earth. Nothing spoke to me audibly, but I became aware of the night, of myself, and of the energy of the earth all around me. It was a seminal moment.

It was not too many years after the rape that my Dad denied me the right to see my grandmother anymore. She was a lesbian, and he did not want me around her. I think she was a lesbian because of all the pain and abuse that she suffered at the houses of relatives where she lived after her mother was killed. Her husband, Granddad George Hammond, who was also her first cousin, would get into big fights with her.

Soon after the rape, Dad took us away. We moved to Kaycee, away from everyone we knew, all our support system. Away from Grandma.

POVERTY

Our family lived near Basin, Wyoming, during my second-grade year. I tried hard to be a little angel, hoping I could be clean again. Hoping I could make my dad proud of me again. That was the year the unemployment checks didn't come when the construction dried up. We were starving, and some church people brought us boxes and boxes of groceries. They didn't preach at us, they didn't lecture. The only reason they found out we needed food was that I passed out at school. I hadn't eaten for two days. When the school nurse asked, I explained our situation.

The school must have told someone, because those church members came over. My dad went and told the other members of the unemployed construction crew, and they came over and took some of the bounty. I remember one lady was about seven months pregnant, and she drank half a gallon of milk in one gulp! At least, that's what it seemed like to me as a little kid.

17

We found all sorts of goodies in those boxes. There was a package of cinnamon rolls, which we ate with baloney on top, and they were so good! Years later, when something bad happened, I would buy a package of rolls and a package of baloney and just eat them in remembrance. It reminded me of the goodness out there.

When I was nine, my parents splurged, buying me a beautiful pair of black patent leather shoes. I was happy about the pretty footwear and wore them on my daily romp through the fields, up the hills, and down by the creek. On my way, I came upon an oily, mud puddle, and without much thought, I walked right through it. Later that afternoon when I came home, my parents vented their frustration on my behind. It was several days before I sat down again.

PARENTS

Now that I think about it, it's amazing I didn't lose my teeth. They didn't rot, and they didn't get knocked out even though I got beaten in the face a lot. Most people who are beaten get their teeth knocked out.

To this day, my teeth are very important to me. Maybe I don't have shampoo for my hair, but I'll figure out a way to get a toothbrush and some toothpaste! When I was fourteen, I had a rotten tooth, and I told the dentist, "You are not going to pull that out!" It's still in my mouth today.

I think my concern about teeth comes from my mother. She had rotten teeth. When she spoke with you, she covered her mouth. She was terrified of doctors and dentists.

Hers is a hard story, too. When she was sixteen, she was raped by the Baptist preacher inside the church. When she was a child, she never knew where she was going to sleep at night. Her dad was a gambler, and her mother would set her under a tree and tell her to wait there while she went to find a place for them to stay that night. She would sit there with her brothers all day waiting for someone to pick them up. They used cardboard for the soles of their shoes.

When Green, her father, left the picture (he was a hustler and no one really knows what happened to him), my Grandmother married Grampa Karspeck. I loved him. He was a gentle soul who adopted and raised all six of the kids in my mom's family in addition to his own. The whole clan of them went to live in Basin, where they farmed sugar beets. Melvin, Mom's older brother, took over the farm when Grampa got too old. The farm is still there and working today.

My mother had beautiful auburn hair until Dad found out that it came out of a bottle. From then on he forbade her to dye it again. He didn't like women because of the abuse he suffered at the hands of his mother. He never let us wear make up – we got into big fights about that.

My dad grew up in a turbulent household, too. Dad was born prematurely and had weak lungs. He used to try to eat breakfast before his parents got in their morning fight because, once the fight began, his parents would hurl the food out into the yard.

Dad's mother abused him, and it's not surprising that he barely tolerated women. He married my mother five days after meeting her in Red Lodge, Montana. My mom was so disappointed when he went out with his buddies two hours after the ceremony and got drunk.

They lost one baby prior to my arrival, and apparently I have a half-sibling somewhere, the result of a one-night-stand my dad had in the service before he got married.

After my sister was born, my mom made him have a vasectomy. She was too scared of doctors to have her tubes tied, but somehow she convinced him to go have the surgery. He came home, waited a few days, and decided he didn't need the help of any doctor. He locked himself in the bathroom and pulled out his own stiches.

He remained faithful, to my mother, though, and she was faithful to him.

My dad smoked three packs of Camels a day until sometime in the mid-Seventies when he saw a program on cigarettes and cancer. That day, he threw out the rest of his cigarettes and never smoked again.

EMPLOYMENT

I had my first job when I was seven years old. It was 1954, and we lived in Kaycee. I scrubbed floors in houses with a cloth and whatever soap the lady of the house had. I brought my little bucket, and the lady would provide the water. I'd get down on my hands and knees and scrub the linoleum. You would only scrub the kitchen and the living room, because the bathroom was outside and the bedroom was private. You were never allowed in bedrooms, even if it was a single lady.

The pay was one dime for each floor. In second grade, I worked each week to earn the dime so I could go to the movies on Saturday. A second floor equaled a soda and a bag of popcorn at the movie. I got the jobs by going around and knocking on doors and asking. It was the only way to get to the movies, since Mom and Dad had enough trouble just trying to feed us.

In third grade, that was 1955, we moved to Riverton, because Dad was following the road construction. We lived at the Cottonwood Cottages, three miles or so upside of town. In the summer, I had a lemonade stand with a friend, and it was pretty successful. We earned five cents a cup, but we still couldn't go to the movies because we lived too far out of town. Instead, we used our money to help buy groceries and school clothes.

In 1956, my fourth grade year, we moved again to Green River. We lived between Rock Springs and Green River in a trailer park. I babysat for twenty-five cents an hour for a family or, sometimes, for two families if one of them ran out to town to do the grocery shopping. One family had two little boys, and the other had a little girl and a little boy about four or five. I just sat and played games with them.

By 1958, we were living in Glen Rock, where we stayed for six months. I quit school at the end of my ninth grade year when I turned sixteen.

"If you're going to quit school, you better have a job!" my dad yelled at me.

"I already quit, and I already have one," I yelled back. I worked for Mrs. Coates at a restaurant where I learned to cook and wait tables. I also worked in a little retail store.

It was at Mrs. Coates' that I first met racism. A black sergeant in a snappy uniform came in to eat one day. I was nice to him. Why not? He had skin and bones like me. Some customers told my dad that I was friendly to the black man, and my dad told me to never be nice to a black person again. He felt the same way about Japanese and Korean people, probably as a result of his service in the Korean War. Later, I would march in Civil Rights demonstrations and marry a man who was half-black.

I remember using my first paycheck to buy my best friend, Betty, her Bermuda shorts outfit. The second check paid for a matching set for me so we could go to the dance together.

Halfway through the year, we moved over to Glendo, and I waited tables at The Hunters' Inn. The owners of the restaurant didn't pay their taxes, and I came to work one day to find the Internal Revenue Service had padlocked the place!

From there, we moved back to Glen Rock where my dad went to work for the county.

THE OCCULT

There was lots of good and lots of evil in those days. The good outweighed the evil, though, until I started opening myself up to the evil and inviting it in. The more I practiced evil, the worse it got.

21

Junior, a thirty-year-old man who lived across the alley from our family in the trailer park, was another one who used me for sex. We were living in Glen Rock, Wyoming. I was fourteen, working outside between our trailers, and he talked me into coming over. From there, it was him giving me things in exchange for sex. I came to understand that I wasn't worth anything except as someone to have sex with.

This man used me for a few months. When you're living in a world where you have been used, raped, or abused, you'd be surprised how easily a predator can talk you into things. Especially when you want to belong.

It was Kay, Junior's ex-wife, who initiated me into the occult.

We drank and partied together, Kay, Junior, and me. We hung out at the Dibble-Dabble Bar. I was only fourteen, but money will buy anything. They would give money to the bartender, and he would turn away when I was drinking.

In the occult world, I belonged. I had power. I could be my own self, unlike the response I got from Christians. Once, when I was ten years old, I wanted to go to church camp at the local Nazarene Church.

"Do you think Jesus Christ would still love me even if I'm not a virgin?" I asked the pastor.

"No," he answered, and told me I was not welcome at his church camp.

If I'm not allowed at church, I thought to myself, *who will accept me?* The answer seemed clear: the devil himself.

If you don't feel loved or accepted, guess what? You'll get involved with evil.

I learned about rituals and practiced them. I learned how to go into meditation states where I could focus and, in doing that, opened myself up to a world in which you can become possessed. And I became possessed. I remember as it grew within me, because I had no feelings. And then, as I performed more rituals, the possession became a solidness, a stoniness where my soul and mind and heart had been. You become like a thing, not a person.

Then you join a group of people involved with the occult in your area. Each group has a leader. The group you're in will send you around and you do whatever they want you to. They send you into churches to find the biggest gossiper. The only thing they want you to do is sow division.

For instance, maybe the air conditioning is broken, and you sit next to the person who gossips all the time and say, "It's really hot in here."

They tell you all about how the air conditioning broke, how they're raising money to replace it, and you say, "But do you see the shoes the pastor is wearing? Or the car he's driving? He spent all the money on himself."

In reality, his shoes were a gift from his mother, his transmission broke, and he borrowed a car from someone in the congregation who owns a dealership, but you have just planted the seeds of division in the most fertile soil. It's not hard to find the gossipers. How many "prayer warriors" are actually "gossip warriors?" They say, "Pray for so-and-so because…" and then they tell things no one needs to hear.

So many men and women in churches are also involved in the occult! It's such a hidden thing, and they are such "good church-goers" no one believes they could be involved in it.

This is my message to people in churches: know your heart. What is your motive? What do you want out of this relationship with God? Are you really there to get attention? Often, that is a person's motivation: attention. What sins are you hiding? Until you get open and honest with yourself and God, until you soften your hard heart, how are you going to pray and fast? People in the occult pray and fast all the time!

People in the occult get up at 2:00 a.m. every day and chant. The devil talks to them the way the Holy Spirit talks to Christians. That's the kind of world they're in.

SELF-WORTHLESS

Martha was a rich girl in my class at school. Her father was the game warden in Glen Rock, Wyoming. In fact, once my dad and brother went out, bagged a deer illegally and got caught by Martha's dad, Dan.

Martha had a birthday party each year for herself and her friends. I was invited to come over and help decorate for the party but was not allowed to stay and participate, because I was not of their social class. When the party was over, I was permitted to help with the clean up and then enjoy a little leftover cake and ice cream with Martha.

This experience is my reference point for feeling inadequate.

Even today, it's because I believe the message reinforced by Martha and her friends – I'm not good enough - that I let people take over my vision, my ideas, even my thoughts. Inside, I feel like I must be the slave of the wealthy or social elite in order to be accepted.

A similar event occurred in eighth grade when I was invited to the prom. Phyllis, my mom's friend that I lived with for awhile, remade an old prom dress for me. While I was in the bathroom at the prom, I heard the "popular kids" talking badly about me. I was so angry I came undone. I chanted a curse on them and made up my mind to take one of those popular girl's boyfriends home with me that night. I did, too.

In Casper, Wyoming, another popular girl had donated a beautiful sweater to The Glass House, a thrift store, where my mother bought it for 35 cents. When I wore it to class, the girl announced it used to be hers. Everyone laughed.

Kids can be very cruel.

That was how I lost some of myself.

So, imagine you're treated this way all the time, and one day a guy comes and tells you how beautiful you are. He gives you gifts and you fall madly in love with him. Then, one day he comes to you and says, "We're a little short of money tonight, so why don't you do this one little sex act for us, so we can get some cash?" And the saga begins. That's how abused or bullied kids get caught in human trafficking.

SNAKES

Our trailer in Glendo was near a creek. I played in the water and liked to catch the garter snakes that lived along the banks. I would take them back to my room and keep them warm in my bed, where they lay dormant as long as they were covered by the blankets.

One day, noticing lumps in my covers, my mom came in to remake my bed after I had gone to school. She twitched back the blankets and out tumbled the drowsy snakes, suddenly alert at the drastic change in temperature. All six slithered off of my bed and dashed into corners of the trailer to hide.

I saw her waiting in the yard when I walked home from school. Before I reached the trailer, she started yelling. She stood in the yard gesticulating wildly until I found every one of those snakes and took them out of the house.

KEEPING COMPANY

In Glendo I worked at a restaurant. On my fourteenth birthday, I took the day off and made myself a cake with purple frosting and took it downtown to share with a friend.

A bunch of boys pulled up in a car and I started talking to them. They told my friend and me that they were hungry, so I went to the restaurant where I worked and bought them a bunch of hamburgers and fries. We all headed over to the lake to celebrate my birthday with a picnic.

We had a great day, just hanging out at the lake. At one point, one of the boys told me they had escaped that morning from the Nebraska State Juvenile Detention Center! Later that afternoon, we went back to Glendo and one of the boys got on the phone and called the Center to tell them where they were.

When the sheriffs arrived and took the boys back into custody, I was hiding under our trailer. My mother was just beside herself. Not long after, we moved back to Glen Rock.

DRINKING

In school and in our neighborhood, I hung out with the people who were old enough to drink. We spent a lot of time drinking. In eighth grade, I didn't work because I was drinking too much. I ran away from home.

When I came back, my mom took me to a psychologist who said there was nothing that could be done for me, and that I would eventually destroy myself. My mother had to pay ninety dollars for me to see that psychologist. She was so angry that the doctor couldn't give her any help after all that money!

"And now I'll have to save for another two years before I can get curtains," she complained.

The psychologist confirmed my understanding that I wasn't worth anything so, "Who cares?" became my philosophy. I became a rebel. People said I was like my Aunt Ardith, who committed suicide at age 24. My parents told me I would be just like her, so when I turned 25 and wasn't dead yet, they couldn't believe it.

RICK E.

The Sixties began with big fights with my dad. He told me I was "just" a woman so I didn't need school because women

26

only had babies and let their husbands use them for sex. So I quit school when I was fifteen and ran away from home again. Those were terrible years.

I found Rick E. on the streets of Douglas. I picked him up and thought my world was going to change for the better. We got drunk and he took me to Big Piney, where we got married. It was 1963, and we were both sixteen years old.

Rick told me he worked on his own ranch. It was true he worked here and there on ranches, but he didn't have his own. It was his aunt's ranch in Big Piney where he took me. I became the cook there and later learned that he put me way out there so he could be off with his girlfriends. He took scissors and cut up all my clothes and then took me to the dumpster and told me that was where I could find clothes from then on.

Once, when he went in to town to go to the bars, I asked to come with him. I was pregnant at the time, and looked it.

"I don't want to be seen with a jersey cow," he snapped, jumping into the truck and peeling out in a cloud of dust. I was seventeen when our son, Shane, was born.

The next year, 1965, David was born. His twin died, but the doctor was able to give me something that saved David. So, I was stuck out on the ranch with two babies and at Thanksgiving Rick went back into town to be with his family. His mother asked where I was, and he said he wasn't bringing me. Virginia, his mom, made him come get me, which was a bad thing because he smacked the hell out of me the whole way in. When we got there, he told me I better not tell anyone.

Rick sold me at least once a week. He spent the money that men paid to have sex with me on booze, girls, nice western shirts, boots, and cowboy hats. After David was born, I shot off Rick's ear with a .30-30 rifle. The only thing that saved his life was that he turned his head. When he heard about it, my dad drove 350 miles to take my gun away from me. I took all Rick's pretty western shirts and squirted syrup on them. He had beaten me so badly.

One of the strange things about Rick was that he wasn't

27

actually all male, but he wasn't all female either. I think part of the reason he was so abusive to women was that he was trying to prove he was a man. His body shape was partially male and partially female. He even had breasts.

He abused the other women he was with, too. Some of these women had people willing to come and rescue them. The last one was Netty. Her folks came from Kansas to get her out of there. One day she and their kids were just gone.

When Shane was born in 1964, Rick and his girlfriend walked into the hospital and said they were going to take the baby as soon as he was released. I told them hell no. Rick really made my life tough after that.

David was born with hydrocephalus and was dying. Rick and his family were jack (non-practicing) Mormons. Virginia called the Elders, who came and anointed David's head with oil and prayed over him. I held that baby the whole way to Children's Hospital in Salt Lake City. That night as we drove, God Almighty performed a miracle in a child. I was the one holding him, and I watched his swollen head get smaller as we drove. When we arrived, they admitted him and found his head had shrunk way down. And, incredibly, there were no lasting effects. As he grew, the only thing he had was a speech impediment. You can still hear it when he gets really tired or excited. He was named after King David. Now he's caught up in alcohol, like so much of my family.

Buffy, our only daughter, was born in June 1967. I only knew her for a year before she was taken from me. Jamey, my youngest son, would be born in 1971 with my second husband.

OUTSIDE OF US

When I was seventeen and giving birth to Shane, I left my body.

To understand what happened, you have to know that at fourteen, I was drinking and dancing on the hood of a car just as

28

the driver put it in gear and lurched forward. I slid off the hood and was struck in the back by the bumper, which wasn't made of plastic like they are today. While I was not badly injured, the impact tilted my uterus to such a degree that Shane's head got stuck as I labored for more than nineteen hours to give birth.

The doctors knew Shane and I were going to die. They called Mom and Dad in Powder River, Wyoming, and told them to come to Douglas, because I was having a baby. They also told my parents not to expect either of us to be alive when they arrived.

Dad's mother, Grandma Nellie Hammond, stormed into the delivery room and threw Doc Johnson up against the wall where she held him by his neck.

"If my granddaughter dies," she told him, "you're gonna die, too." My grandma had a reputation in Douglas. There was not a man who could whip her. She was a strong, strong lady. She could go out on the prairie and yank up a sagebrush with her bare hands. She died in 1967.

Doc Johnson lost no time in calling for Dr. Crenshaw, who drove in from Casper a few minutes later with his dad's forceps in his hand. He locked them onto Shane's head and pulled. Shane still has the scars.

I had been in hard labor for hours. When Dr. Crenshaw put those forceps up there and locked them, my body gave out and my heart stopped beating. Dr. Crenshaw yelled for Dr. Johnson to start massaging my heart while he pulled Shane out.

I left my body and watched them work on me. I felt totally free. Nothing mattered. I certainly did not want to go back.

As I watched, my dad came flying through the doors of the delivery room yelling, "What's going on?"

At that same moment, I was pulled back toward my body, and there was a knowing, an inner voice saying, "You need to go back. There is more you need to experience and do."

As if pulled by a vacuum, I got sucked back down through my head.

My dad, yelling. Shane being pulled. My heart beating. I was back.

To this day, part of me is detached from the material world. I go through turmoil, but I have a different view of things because of the way this experience changed me.

Sometimes, when I am totally alone and quiet, I will meditate and feel that freedom again. It comes back to me. I have absolutely no fear of death. None at all. In fact, I don't believe there is any death. We just change. The body dies, but really, our body is dying every day. Changing every day. I am not the same body I was when I was ten years old.

To me, there is no death. My sadness when someone's dies is because I can't touch them anymore. I have no fear of death itself, because to me it's simply a dimension change. You come out of this body and are sucked back to God, like a caterpillar who makes a cocoon and then bursts out! The thing about death is that I don't want a lot of pain.

I know I'm not the only person who has a remembrance of things before birth. It's not that I've spoken to other people about it, or them to me. We understand that we don't talk about it or we'll end up in the psych ward being fed pills. But I know I'm not "out there" by myself.

Angels? I see angels all the time. I've always seen the angels. Once, at an intersection, I came up behind a car and actually saw the energy between our cars. My car just stopped.

Sometimes I wake up and it seems as if someone is kissing my cheek. I look for a cat or feel for fuzz that might have brushed against me, but nothing is physically there. It's the angels. They speak to me through my intuition. They've always been with me. I don't take the angels for granted. I don't take God for granted. I have more of a *knowing* than a believing.

One result of my faith, my *knowing* God, is that I don't know what jealousy feels like. I don't know what greed feels like, or selfishness. I just have this community-mindedness that I've had all my life. On the ranch, if my mother gave me a peanut butter sandwich, then I always gave some of it to a bird

30

or the workhorse. People tell me that this kind of sharing gets me in trouble.

Besides not being jealous, I do not envy anyone. For instance, if I don't have anything at all and someone gets something, I never feel that feeling of *I wish I had that.*

The community-mindedness runs in our family. Shane, Buffy, David, Jamey, and their kids, with all their challenges, are involved in helping the community. My brother and sister are, too. My brother is a businessman who takes good care of his employees. My sister is a compassionate person, always taking care of people's animals.

I do feel depressed sometimes, but I never stay that way. I might feel sad about something, but all you have to do is give me a couple of hours and it's done.

RANCH WORK

In 1966, I was pregnant again, but Rick beat me so badly that I lost that baby. Then, I went to work in Big Piney at a little store as a retail clerk. When I got pregnant again, I went to work on another ranch. I fed 150 head of cattle every morning, helped with the calving, built fences, and was snowed in for the whole winter. I knew the moose and deer were going to come eat at the haystacks, so I shot a moose with a neighbor's gun so we would have something to eat.

Working at another ranch, I'd get up at two or three o'clock in the morning and make breakfast of biscuits with gravy, eggs, bacon, and steaks for the forty ranch hands. Then I'd make lunch and supper and clean up. I'd go to bed at 1:00 a.m. and then get up and do it all again. Seven days a week. I took a nap during the afternoon, and I didn't have to clean the house. There was a housekeeper for that. I'd get supper going – maybe a roast – and put it on to cook really slowly. Then I'd take my nap.

Lunch was easy, though. You'd stop and think, *what can*

they take on horseback? You're taking biscuits and beef jerk. The ranch hands didn't really stop for lunch. They'd be out on the fence line. They'd rest on the horse or maybe get off for ten or fifteen minutes, but they weren't going to get off and take half an hour to eat because they have hundreds of miles of fences to check or fix. And you'd better have a good supper when they get back! They're really going to eat!

You know, I enjoyed that. It was fun putting that food together, making sure there was enough and organizing it so it all comes off the stove at the same time.

I remember one six-month summer job that Rick and I did at a ranch in Box Elder Canyon. We were building a fence, and had the two boys with us. They let us stay in a little log cabin without any furniture. It had nothing in it except mice, hundreds and hundreds of mice. We built a little fire and slept around it with the boys so the mice wouldn't crawl up on us. Rick had a .22 rifle and would shoot the mice at night. This cabin was out on the prairie where no one had been for years and years, so we were just kind of camping out. It was really interesting.

When I was pregnant with Buffy, who was born in 1967, I got up at 4:00 a.m. every morning. We had to pitch the hay on the wagon or sled. I would put those two little boys on that wagon, and we would go out and feed one hundred fifty head of cattle. It took three wagons full, so we were out most of the day.

In the spring, I was really pregnant with Buffy at calving time. One of the heifers was having a hard time birthing her calf, so I flagged down the county road construction guys and had them help me pull the calf. I was so big! We got the heifer into the barn and saw that the calf was too big for her, so we wrapped chains around the feet of the calf that were sticking out of its mama. One guy sat on the heifer's head, I put my legs against the cow, and the other sat behind me and used me as a lever. Together, we pulled that calf and saved the cow!

Rick was in town getting drunk with his girlfriend.

The county guys told the ranch owner in town that I was

32

taking care of things, not Rick, so Rick was fired and we were done at ranches. I dug ditches, cleaned motel rooms, washed dishes in a cafe, whatever I could do to get money for food, drugs, and alcohol.

MORMON CONVERSION

We were in Kemmerer, Wyoming, at Rick's Grandmother Neilson's house when I started having to go pee all the time, so I kept going to the outhouse. Finally, I told Rick we'd better go to the hospital. We got there in time for the nurse to catch Buffy. The doctor came running in after she was born!

Rick's Mom watched the other children while I went to have Buffy. She tolerated me but didn't like me. She liked her grandkids and her son, but not me.

After Buffy's birth, Rick disappeared for nine months. I lived on nothing in a trailer house in Kemmerer, Wyoming. It was December, just before Christmas, and we had eaten all the food my mother-in-law had delivered. There was no food but the sour milk that I was feeding to the kids. The water was frozen right down the pipes into the ground, and there was no heat. I was watching the movie The Birds when there was a knock at the door, and there were two Mormon missionary ladies who said they wanted to tell me about Jesus Christ. I told them to come in and let *me* tell *them* about Jesus. And I did. I really did.

The next day, the Mormons showed up and moved the trailer to another spot. They gave me food, got me heat, and brought diapers for the baby. They took really good care of us, and I was happy.

I decided to be baptized Mormon. With all the love and help they gave me, of course I wanted to be a part of it! I will never forget walking into the Mormon Visitor's Center in Salt Lake City, and there was the wide sky and the huge statue of Jesus Christ with his beautiful eyes. I fell at his feet.

Two months later, Rick showed up. I wasn't having him, but his mother, Virginia, came to convince me to take him back. She knew he was beating me, but she said I deserved it. He promised me that he had changed and that we needed to get away from both of our families.

"We need to live somewhere else and we can be married in the Temple and go to church together," he told me. He had been in Oregon the whole time.

CASPER

Rick moved us to Casper, Wyoming, in 1968. I was working at the Green Derby restaurant from 10:00 p.m. to 7:00 a.m., and he was working at a filling station from 8:00 AM until 5:00 PM. Rick watched the kids while I was working and I watched them during the day. A neighbor helped when one of us didn't get home on time. It worked well.

One slow night, I left work early and went home. I showed up an hour before I was supposed to and found the kids asleep but Rick gone. I discovered that he left each night half an hour after I did so he could spend time with his girlfriend, who had moved down from Oregon to Casper. That was the real reason he had moved us.

When I found this out, we had a big fight. He and his girlfriend took the kids and said they were going to Big Piney. I didn't have a vehicle or the energy to follow them. I was just tired. Later, I found out that they took the kids to Glen Rock and dropped them off with my parents. I didn't even know my parents had them. Even though taking kids out of their home is bad for them, our kids would have been much worse off with Rick, so it turned out to be a good thing that they ended up with my parents.

THE TOMAHAWK ROOM

In August 1968, a few weeks after Rick took off, I was still working at the Green Derby. It was County Fair time, so I was making good tips and trying to figure out what to do next. I had to walk to work because I didn't have a car. To be there by 10:00 p.m. I left the apartment at 9:00 p.m.

One night, some girls came into the restaurant and told me there was a better way to do things, a way that involved earning a lot more money. They took me to the Towson Hotel and introduced me to Renee Laird, who owned the hotel and ran the Tomahawk Room. She interviewed me and wanted to see me dance in a western outfit. I took my tip money and bought a white hat, a pair of white boots, a green metallic western shirt, a matching vest, and pants.

When I showed up that night to dance for her, I was dressed in my new clothes.

"You can't dance in that," she said, eyeing me from hat to boots.

"But you told me I had to have a cowboy outfit," I argued.

"Yes," said Renee, "but I thought you understood what kind of dancing I want you to do." She took me to the bathroom and made me strip everything off. Then she handed me a pair of black net stockings, my boots, the green metallic vest, and my cowboy hat.

The audition, I found out, was in front of the Tomahawk Room patrons. I got on the stage and stood there while the music started. My stomach was cramping up with stage fright. The bartender reached over and handed me a glass, and by the time that whiskey hit my stomach, I was dancing.

Renee Laird ran the hotel, the bar, and the dancers, but she was a very caring woman. She taught me how to dance on stage, and I felt like she was looking out for me. All the dancers felt that way, although Renee was also very strict about her rules. There were guards stationed upstairs by the hotel rooms.

If we wanted to entertain guys, we had to do it outside.

One night, I was with a guy, and we were so drunk and high that I told him he didn't have the guts to shoot me with his 12-gauge shotgun. He did. He pulled the trigger and shot me full of rock salt.

"You really shot me!" I yelled.

"I guess I did," he roared back, surprised. We were that stoned and drunk.

Renee Laird was the one who took care of me. She had me lay down and using a pair of tweezers, she pulled the rock salt out of my belly and legs.

"I'll take care of you, Penny," she told me, rubbing lotion into the cuts, "but next time don't be so stupid!"

Renee owned a horse farm outside of Douglas, Wyoming, on the road to Laramie Peak. In later times, I went out there and visited her before she died of breast cancer. We laughed and giggled about things that happened at the Tomahawk Room. Renee told me she had been grooming me to run the whole hotel so she could move to Cheyenne and start a new venture. It didn't work, though, because I ran off and she contracted breast cancer. She didn't have any family or children and never married the guy who helped her run the hotel.

I went to visit my parents about three weeks after Rick left, and found my kids there. My dad was mad at me for going back to Rick to begin with, and he wasn't going to let me out of my responsibilities.

"You're the one who had these kids, you're going to take care of them. You made this bed, you're going to sleep in it," he said, glaring at me.

I took the kids back to Casper with me, and they stayed in a little loft where the girls and I had babysitters to watch our children while we were dancing. Of the fifteen dancers, thirteen of them had children, so most of the time there would be four babysitters up there. Those girls were all dancing to support their kids.

The girls and me would practice our routines up in that

loft where the kids were. Shane, at four-years-old, was watching and learning. Young kids watch every move you make, and they learn. That's why I'm always telling people, "Your kids are sponges! They absorb!"

Years later, who was the most popular dancer in the gay bars of Tulsa, Oklahoma? My son Shane.

"Mom, you're the one who taught me," he says.

MY PARENTS FIND OUT

One night while I was dancing on stage, a shrill voice cut through the music.

"Penny Kay! What are you doing?"

It was my mother.

The whole bar stopped. Even the music stopped. The bartender just pulled the plug on the jukebox. Everyone in the room froze. Each one of us felt like we had been caught by our mothers.

I put on a wrap and came out of the Tomahawk Room to meet her.

"What are you doing here, Mom?"

"Your Dad and I came up to borrow some money. He's in the lobby. Where are my babies?" My mother was furious.

"Upstairs with a babysitter."

"Don't you ever say anything to your dad about what you're doing here. You and me will talk about it later." Her eyes flashed.

"I have to make a living, Mom."

She pursed her lips and turned away. When she faced me again, it was through tears. "Don't *ever* tell your dad," she hissed.

After my mother left, the atmosphere in the Tomahawk Room was different for the rest of the night. People went home early and I couldn't get my rhythm back. Neither could any of the girls.

Another time, I got drunk after the show and woke up in a trailer. When I opened the door, I saw the trailer was in the middle of a construction zone in Kaycee, and there, a little way down, was my dad!

I jumped out of the trailer and grabbed the foreman and told him to get me out of there. He tried to kid with me, but I told him I was Darr Hammond's daughter. His face changed and he threw me in a truck and drove me back to Casper really fast!

Later, when my Dad was dying, he said to me, "Tell me about the day when you was on the construction site in your costume and thought I didn't see you. Tell me about the dancing." He knew all those years and never said a word.

LOSING THE KIDS

I learned more than dancing at the Tomahawk Room. They taught me how to bartend, and I also ran the little lunch cafe. Sometimes, Renee would get jobs for us dancers in other places. Once, she found us a week-long gig at the Mint Bar in Roundup, Montana. They liked me so much they asked me to stay for a second week. It was my personality that made them want me to stay. The others were prettier, but I ended up being the star because of my personality.

My best friend in Casper offered to watch my kids while I stayed the second week. While I was gone, she got tired of taking care of them and dropped them off at the Natrona County Welfare Office where the Director of Welfare and the assistant, his girlfriend, stole the three of them. They sold a lot of poor people's kids. Shane, David, and Buffy went to the highest bidder. Unfortunately, the mother died six months later, and the kids went back to foster care. Then they went to a second couple that divorced almost immediately, sending them back to foster care again. Finally, they were adopted by a couple whose official adoption application had been rejected. The treatment they received is the stuff of nightmares.

38

When I came back, I managed to see the kids because they were still in Casper, but I couldn't get my hands on them or deal with the situation. My mother and younger sister, Patty, set out for Casper with the intention of bringing the children back to their house in Douglas, but the bus driver did not see them where they stood in the shelter and kept on driving. When my mom and sister missed that bus, my children missed their chance at a safe childhood.

LEADERSHIP

I was such a little leader. Now, I had lost my children and I was an angry leader.

"Who cares?" I raged.

At this point I had a boyfriend who was younger than me. I decided that we should be Bonnie and Clyde. A bunch of teens went with us to Chugwater, Wyoming, and saw a lady start her car and leave it running in her driveway to warm up. We jumped into it and drove over the border to Denver, Colorado, where the transmission went out.

A thirteen-year-old girl was with us. I shoved her into a police car telling them she was a runaway. Then I took off.

My boyfriend volunteered to go back over the border into Wyoming to get something for me. I warned him not to cross the state line because of the car we had stolen and a bunch of checks we had forged. He said he'd be careful, but he never came back. They nabbed him when he crossed the border and put him in juvenile detention, since he was a minor. He served eighteen months.

Years later, I saw him again.

"I did it all for you," he said.

I knew better than to cross back into Wyoming, so I took the other kids who were with us and went north into Montana and Idaho. I found a new boyfriend who suddenly started asking to borrow my mascara. He went from straight to gay, just like that.

I handled all this stress by going to a party and getting so drunk and drugged that I blacked out. When I woke up, I was in Denver without any identification, and a black pimp was beating the hell out of me. His job was to beat me into submission. By the time he's done, a girl thinks it's her fault. Then, two black girls took me into a store to teach me how to steal clothes so I could have something to wear.

PROSTITUTION IN DENVER 1969-1970

In prostitution, it's just a job. You dissociate. You have no feelings. You ask no names, and you don't tell yours. You just do the job and get paid. It's strictly business.

One night, one of the johns (customers) bought me and took me to a sleazy hotel. He gave me my money up front, like he had to, and I gave him my usual line.

"What's your pleasure?"

But instead, he said, "I want to talk to you."

"Okay," I replied, not sure what to think.

"Why are you here? You don't have the heart of a prostitute." I told him a little of my story and how I was stuck with this pimp who guarded me all the time. The man thought for awhile and then said, "I'll be back tomorrow night and buy you again. Then, I'll get you out of town."

True to his word, he came back the next night and did everything we planned. Even though I was drunk and stoned, he managed to get me out of the room without the pimp seeing me. He drove me across Denver to another bar, took me inside and told the bartender to give me whatever I wanted to drink.

"She needs to leave *tonight*," he told the bartender, and then walked out.

To this day, I have no idea who this man was. We didn't even have sex.

The bartender told me to get close to a guy he pointed

out, a truck driver with a bunch of money named CJ. That night, CJ and his truck-driving partner had stopped at the bar, but the partner took all CJ's money, so CJ took me out to his truck where we crawled up into the sleeper and slept off our drunk.

The next morning, I heard his partner in the front seat bad-mouthing "that dirty little whore" from the night before. CJ pulled back the curtain and pointed at me, annoyed.

"You mean her? She's coming with us." CJ never told me he had a wife and kids in Milwaukee.

The truck was United Van Lines and was going to Maine, so I went all the way with them and helped unload furniture in the middle of winter. The gentleman we were moving was in the Armed Forces and had a 100-inch long couch. No one could figure out how we were going to get it up to the tenth floor in the elevator, so I suggested we take it up the stairs. We did, and each one of us got a $100 tip. That tip made CJ decide to keep me, so I learned to move furniture. I was his helper and his sex partner.

In 1970, we finished a contract for North American Van Lines in Sioux Falls, South Dakota. We planned to travel across the United States moving furniture. I thought this would be the way I would spend the rest of my life. My kids were gone, the world had no promise, and I was feeling really sick.

I went to the doctor, who said, "Congratulations!"

That was Jamey.

After Buffy, I truly believed I would never get pregnant again. Incredibly, despite all the sex trafficking, the only sexually transmitted disease I contracted was from CJ. Technically, though, he was the one who tested positive. I tested negative.

CJ went out driving truck, but I was too sick to go, so I stayed behind in Sioux Falls and worked at a cafe waiting tables for a while. Then we moved to Vermillion, South Dakota, where I was still too sick to work. Our apartment was above a doctor's office and I would crawl down the stairs every day and get a shot of something from the doctor to make me feel better. I would just lie on the couch while CJ was out driving truck.

FAMILY TRADITIONS

I made a trip back to Wyoming to see Mom and Dad even though I was still wanted for the car-stealing incident. CJ wouldn't marry me until all the mess was cleared up, so Dad got Jim Fagan to be my lawyer. We stood in front of the judge, who glared at me and then at my dad.

"When is your family ever going to learn?" he demanded. My granddad had stood in front of him, my dad had stood in front of him, and now it was me.

In spite of everything, there are no records anywhere that show that I was ever charged with anything. I should have been in prison many times. That is the hand of God at work.

FLORIDA

By 1971, Jamey was six months old and we had a brand new trailer home in Sioux City, Iowa. It was really nice. My mom and dad even came to visit us for Thanksgiving. My neighbors in the trailer park agreed to watch Jamey, so after Thanksgiving, I went to work at Zenith, putting together televisions. CJ drove truck and I worked. Jamey was two years old when things changed again.

One evening, a phone call came in.

"Hello?" I answered.

"Uh, is CJ there?" The woman's voice was unsteady.

"No. He's not here until later tonight."

"Well, I don't know what I'm going to do," she wailed.

"Why?" I asked.

"Because I'm eight-months pregnant with CJ's baby, and I don't have anywhere to go."

I picked her up and brought her back to the trailer, fed

42

her, packed my bag and Jamey's. Then I called my buddy from Zenith, a mixed-race man named Jim H., who had introduced me to mainline heroin.

"Hey, Jim," I said, "you still wanna go to Florida?"

That night I picked up CJ from work and talked to him on the way home like I always did. We walked through the door, and there she was. He looked at her and then at me.

"It's your problem," I shrugged. I took Jamey, got in the Mark One Mustang, picked up Jim and his male friend, and drove to Orlando. Divorce followed. It was 1973.

ANOTHER HUSBAND

For the next seven years, I lived in and around Orlando. My first job was at Walgreens where I met a man from India, Kushal T., whom I agreed to marry so he could become a citizen. In thanks, his mother gave me a beautiful ruby bracelet that I hawked for fifty bucks to buy heroin.

Next, I worked in a factory. One day, I called in sick, drove to Tampa so Kushal could become a citizen, and was back in time for Jim to pick me up from work.

MISTY

The years I spent in Florida, I was into hardcore drugs.

I remember being on the Orange Blossom Trail, shooting up and being so tired of the whole scene. I said, "I'm never going to do this again," and threw my outfit, my drug paraphernalia, onto the highway.

Later, I was sick and desperate for a fix. I got down on my hands and knees in the middle of highway traffic trying to find my outfit so I could get another hit.

Misty was my best friend in Florida. We did heroin together and hung around together. I was the one who went first when we shot up. One time, she wanted to go first, so I helped her. Within forty-five seconds, she was dead. She looked at me and died in my arms. What she injected was called a Hot Shot – but the dealer cut the heroin with way too much strychnine, and it killed her almost instantly. When you buy, you just don't know what you're getting.

I had to go back to the same dealer to get my fix.

He looked at me and didn't care.

BACK TO WYOMING

National Cash Register hired me at a time when I was moving around a lot. I started having severe pain in my abdomen so I went to the Orlando Hospital for what turned out to be a pelvic infection. The doctors told me they found cancer cells on my cervix and that I should have a complete hysterectomy.

When I told my mother, she insisted that I come home and have the operation done by Dr. Homer in Douglas, Wyoming. Doc Homer had no toes because he froze his feet one winter night when he was out on the prairie trying to save his cattle. Without toes, he had bad balance, so to stabilize himself he wore cowboy boots everywhere he went – even into the operating room!

The operation was a success, but afterwards, I didn't have any hormones in my body. Doc Homer didn't realize how fast I would go into menopause.

As the hormones drained away, I went crazy. I sat there cradling a .30-30 rifle while Jim and Jamey ran to get my dad.

Even being possessed with a demon is nothing like the feeling of insanity you get when you don't have any hormones in your body. There is no drug that compares. A serial killer has a rationalization, but if you have no hormones, there's no rationalization. My dad, with PTSD from the Korean War, found me on the floor with fixed, wide eyes. He crawled slowly forward until he was close enough to snatch me in a bear hug while Jim wiggled the gun out of my hands and got me to the hospital where they started injecting me with horse urine, Premarin, to stabilize me. I remember that feeling so well. I even wanted to kill Jim and Jamey.

In retrospect, I wonder why they recommended a complete hysterectomy instead of at least leaving my ovaries to make hormones? I wonder if someone at the Orlando hospital made a decision to take away my fertility because I was a 24-year-old heroin addict who already had four children?

I stayed in Douglas for a full year after the hysterectomy, working at the Douglas Rest Home as the morning cook. It was fun to work with the residents there. The work was good, and I did things to make the residents happy, like cooking heart-shaped pancakes on Valentine's Day.

On the side, I prostituted and sold drugs.

I was also heavily involved in the occult. One of my co-workers did something that made me really mad at her. I told her I was going to put a curse on her.

I made a doll and put a bunch of pins in it and left it on her desk. Within ten minutes of seeing that doll, she went home throwing-up. She was sick for a month. I hadn't cursed her, but she thought I did. That story illustrates the power of suggestion.

TWO HUSBANDS AT ONCE

Jim H. married me in Douglas. He didn't know about Kushal, but my mother did. She didn't come to the wedding because she knew I was already married. The shame I felt was subconscious, but strong enough that I packed Jamey's and my bags and got out of Douglas. I told Jim he didn't have to come, but he did. My parents were disappointed in me when I told them I was sorry, but just couldn't stay.

The day I left Douglas was my day off work. I drove straight from Wyoming to my pusher in Orlando and put a needle in my arm. Jamey didn't see it. He never saw me shoot up, but he did watch me drink and smoke pot.

Not long after, I got in a big, hairy fight with Jim over money and heroin. He left. It was just a mess.

I went back to a great job at NCR and danced in two bars on the side. One was where I had first met my friend, Misty. That first week I went back to work at NCR, I was so stoned from powerful Turkish hashish I ended up in the hospital. When I woke up, I called CJ's mother and begged her to send CJ to pick up Jamey. I knew he was the one who was getting hurt the most. CJ came, and I promised to take Jamey back in six months. He seemed to understand, but when he and his girlfriend took our son that day in 1975, they went to Mexico, and I didn't see Jamey again until he was ten years old.

I had a thing going for one of the managers at NCR. I used to go to his boat in the marina and spend the night with him. One night, an overwhelming feeling came over me that I don't even have words to describe. The best I can do is to say that I was suddenly aware of the hugeness of God's love for me. I was smothered in the realization that God loved me in spite of where I was and what I was doing.

I turned to the man and asked, "Are you Jesus Christ?" Of course, he wasn't, but I didn't know where that feeling, that knowledge came from. Someone was praying for me. Maybe someone who didn't even know me. The same way God will wake me up in the middle of the night to pray for someone in Russia. I don't know them, I don't know the situation, I just know that God is using me to intercede for someone.

This is the way God works. His spirit is moving all over, all the time. When he finds a heart open, he goes in. If the heart isn't cracked enough yet, he comes back later and tries again. Your heart has to be open before his Spirit can get in. Often, people have to get to rock bottom before they can call for help from God. Before their hearts are open enough to accept his help.

There is no doubt it is God who does the moving.

Otherwise, how could someone in a sinful lifestyle ever get turned around? They get out of the mess by God touching them. There is no other answer but God. When you're at the very bottom and there is no one on the earth who can fix you and touch you, you finally say, "God, will you help me?"

This movement of God happened just before a series of events that led to my getting clean and sober. God knew I needed to be scrubbed in mind and body before he could use me for his purpose.

Not long afterward, the shift supervisor at NCR found me totally stoned on the floor, so I lost my job.

PROSTITUTION ON THE ROAD

The next thing that came my way was a job being sold by a pimp to truckers. The pimp would sell me to a trucker, I would get in the truck, and the pimp would follow the trucker in a car. I would do my job while the trucker drove. This happens all the time. If you see a truck suddenly weave, you know what's probably going on. When I was done, we'd pull into a truck stop and my pimp would sell me to the next guy.

So I went from one coast to another.

Around my birthday in 1978, I was caught prostituting in New Jersey.

The police called my dad. He told them his daughter had died years ago.

The pimp disappeared when he saw the cops all around me. I had no ID, no nothing. A trucker, who happened to be standing at the truck stop, paid the cops and said he'd take responsibility for me. Kenny threw me in his truck and we left. He took me to Minneapolis and kicked me out on the street. I had no shoes and no ID. I found the street people, then a boyfriend with a place where I could crash.

MINNEAPOLIS

In Minneapolis, I went to work at Banner Engineering making the scanners that open doors. My personality made people like me, and Amy hired me. I was stoned all the time, but they didn't fire me because I always showed up on time. Until I got my first paycheck and could use the buses, I had to walk and hitchhike all the way to work in Golden Valley, which was twenty-three miles round trip.

In the meantime, my boyfriend kept taking the money I gave him to buy my pills and using it to buy alcohol for himself. Once, when I caught him, I was not a happy camper, and he knew he was going to be in trouble with me. I tore down to get him from his Alcoholics Anonymous (AA) meeting, and in the process met the leaders, Dick and Lois K. They told me there is a better way to live than drinking and drugging.

From then on, I went to AA at 2218A Clubhouse Street every Monday. The food money I saved by eating their donuts and coffee left me more to spend on drugs. Before long, my boyfriend and I had another fight, so I called Dick and Lois and told them I was ready to go into 30-day treatment. The real reason I called was so that I could lock the house and keep my boyfriend from being able to get in for thirty days. That would teach him a lesson.

Dick and Lois picked me up from a friend's house after I shot, drank, and snorted everything I had in the house.

Banner Engineering agreed to hold my job while I was away on my "leave of absence."

While this was all happening, I was still involved with the occult, doing witchcraft, casting spells and things like that. I had done it all through my childhood and youth, and now I went into treatment doing it.

CRAZINESS ON THE 6TH FLOOR

When they took me to the hospital, I went through a

physical and mental detox. When alcoholics go into rehab, they can have meds that help them with the withdrawal, because alcohol withdrawal can kill you fast. At that time, drug addicts like me, though, had to come off cold turkey. So in detox, I lost it mentally. They took me to the psych ward on the sixth floor.

There, I spoke to an imaginary deer. The psychologist said because the deer is a real animal, he was able to talk to me through it. It was an anchor that kept me in the real world. If I had seen a monster or something imaginary, I might not have come back.

It was a little more than a week before I got my head back. My mother said I called her collect every day and her phone bill was more than a thousand dollars. Daddy was so angry. Later, she told me that in those calls she would tell me to listen to the doctor.

I convinced every patient on the sixth floor that the staff was poisoning us. None of us ate. We insisted that we needed pizza and that the pizza guys had to deliver it to the ward. They did, too! The psychologist wrote a little book about me called, *The Miracle Child.*

When I was released from the sixth floor, I went back down to the fourth floor with the others in Rehab.

At the time, I believed I was the daughter of Satan, so I cursed people on the fourth floor. I got a group of patients to believe that we were followers of Satan and that I could do anything. I really believed what people had been telling me – that I was bad, worthless, and evil.

Carol, my counselor in treatment, was only a couple of years older than me. She was sick of hearing me talk about how powerful I was, so one day she said to me, "If you're so powerful, change the fall leaves back to green." That got me thinking.

I knelt by my bed in the treatment center and prayed, "If there is a God, tell me where my kids are. I don't want to interfere in their lives, just know where they are. If you tell me,

I'll stay clean."

I stayed in rehab for nine weeks.

God kept his side of the bargain, and so did I.

MY SPONSORS

It was through me that my counselor, Carol, met Dick and Lois, my AA sponsors. Carol helped Lois through some difficult family situations. It devastated Lois when Carol died of cancer in 2009. Then Dick died, too. He had a little twinge in July 2011, about three weeks after his son died of kidney cancer. He went to the doctor for a check up and they found he had the same fast-moving kidney cancer. He was dead by December.

I spoke to him on the phone before he died. He told me not to come out from West Virginia to Minneapolis to see him. The cancer was so fast moving he was sure he'd be in a semi-coma by the time I arrived. I did go up for the memorial service, though. Many of the people from our AA group were still alive, and it really helped me to see them.

Dick helped hundreds of people through AA, but he told me I was his special story, and after me, he died. It seems like I am the last assignment people have to do. When I look back, it's like all the people who helped me make significant changes in my life have died.

AFTER TREATMENT

When I left the hospital, Dick and Lois took me back to my house to get my few belongings. Seeing the place through sober eyes, I could hardly believe that my 'palace,' with American Flag curtains and stolen street sign decorations, was such a roach motel.

I went to live at Wayside Halfway House. After my first week there, I went back to work at Banner. I taught the

50

company managers about alcoholism and drug addiction and how their picnics and company get-togethers only attracted the same core people because they were coming for the alcohol. I became the activity director and started holding talent shows. Everyone started coming to the picnics, even families, because alcohol was no longer served.

Through my teaching, the CEO came to understand that his teenage daughter was a closet alcoholic. Company managers all went to classes at Mercy Hospital to learn about alcoholism. A new company policy was defined: all alcoholics, or those who lived with them, would have the opportunity to go to treatment before they lost their jobs. I trained the Vietnamese workers using pictures. I wrote training manuals. Morale and productivity began to rise.

I asked Amy why she hired me originally. She said she saw something in me that nobody else saw. Under my rough exterior, there was a compassionate person who needed to be let out. Banner Engineering spent ten thousand dollars to help me get sober.

I took my week of vacation from Banner soon after treatment so I could go home and visit my parents. The last time they had seen me, I was a strung out hippie, covered in rings, beads, gaudy make up, and unkempt hair. When I got off the plane in a suit with neatly styled hair and modest make-up, my mom and dad didn't even recognize me. I walked past and then circled around and stood behind them, listening to them deliberate over whether or not I would really be clean and sober. They saw the change in me that week.

The first five years of sobriety are full of turmoil while you change habits, friends, and entertainment. When you start using alcohol and drugs, your mind stops growing even if your body keeps on. When you get sober, you have to play catch up in your mentality. When I got sober in 1979, I was 37 years old. My mental age, though, was about thirteen, and I had to go back through my teen years again. I behaved so much like a teenage girl that I had a boyfriend, Scott, who was 16 years old!

After the halfway house, I first lived in a working-women's dormitory, and then with James. Because James was gay and had a boyfriend, I got my very own bedroom.

BANK FRAUD

When I moved downtown to the working-women's dormitory, I was doing really well. I had a few different boyfriends, but I was sober and stayed off drugs. When you first get sober, they recommend you not have any serious relationships for five years while you ride the waves of your new life.

Next thing I knew, I was doing just the opposite. I met a nice, good-looking guy who turned out to be trouble. At the time, there was no diagnosis for my bipolar disorder, but in retrospect, I see how manic I was while we were together. We worked out two fraud schemes, just for the fun of it.

In the first, I would tell the ATM I was depositing a $500 check in it when in fact, it was a blank piece of paper in the envelope. An hour later, I would come back to the ATM and drawn out $300 in cash against my "deposit."

My boyfriend had access to the checks at a large payroll corporation. He heard me telling stories about committing check fraud in Wyoming, so he asked me to help him forge checks. He would steal a bundle of them from work and deliver them to me. I practiced official signatures to perfection, signed the checks, and handed them off to be deposited by other people throughout the city.

They caught me when the electronic signature reader picked up a tiny dot I accidentally made, but not until I had forged many thousands of dollars worth of checks.

I went to jail for a weekend, but because they did not charge me in time, I walked out, much to the chagrin of the detectives. When I went in front of the judge, he opted to give me a year in "hard-core" Gestalt counseling rather than prison.

Treatment was nothing compared to that counseling. The hardest part was having to be honest with everyone, including the leadership at Banner, about my check and ATM thefts.

During those same first five years of sobriety, I also defrauded the IRS by claiming my fish and the butterflies outside my window as dependents. I owed more than $30,000 in back taxes, and since I couldn't pay, they came and took everything I owned and sold it to offset my debt. They left me one single change of clothes.

It is another example of the hand of God that I was in Minnesota, the state that pioneered treatment for alcoholic criminals. It was another miracle that I never went to prison. Through all of these events, Banner Engineering, who listened to what I taught them about the behavior of addicts, was able to uncover and stop long-standing, drug-related industrial espionage. Which just goes to show how God takes what looks bad and uses it for good.

FORTUNE-TELLING

My best friend from AA was Marsha K. We spent a lot of time together, and she was worried about me. When she heard about the ATM and check business, she brought me a little statue to watch over me and keep me safe.

One day, as we were walking downtown, she suggested we visit a new fortune-teller who had set up shop on the street. I shrugged and followed her inside. The "seer" specialized in reading a person's future through the features of the face, and in a few minutes, she was telling Marsha all the things that would happen to her in the coming years. When they were finished, Marsha turned to me.

"Your turn, Penny," she said, but the fortune-teller just glared at me.

"I'm not touching you," she spat. "You belong to God, and I won't touch you."

That taught me where fortune telling comes from.

Mom, Dad, Granddad, Aunt Ardith, 1940s

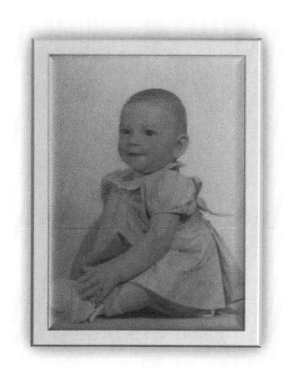

My brother, Darr Dwayne

My sister, Patty

Me, age 5 months, with my mom.

Mom, me, and a cousin

Riding a tricycle, age three

Age four

Back row, center
Age six, after the rape

Age seven years

Age nine years

Riverton, WY

Playing dress-up

**I'm on the right, already taking care of
people**

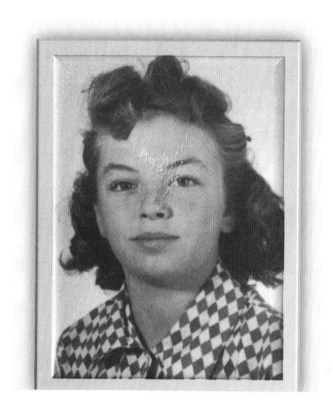

Age twelve years

Rick E., my first husband with our children:

(L-R) Buffy, David, and Shane, 1967

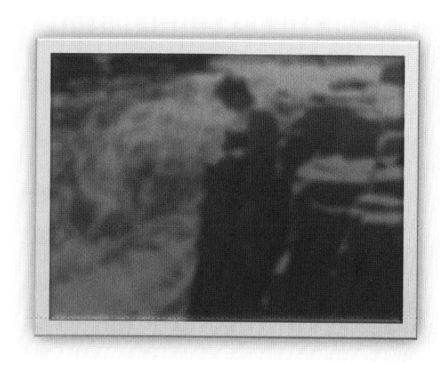

My second
husband, CJ, 1971

Jamey, 1971

67

Jim H., my third husband, 1973

Florida: L - my license, 1974 ; C – Jamey and me; R – Misty and her boyfriend

My parents, Shirley and Darr
Hammond, in the early 1980s

My dad, just prior to his death
in 1983

70

Minneapolis, 1980

MCC Graduation, 1984

Banner Engineering, 1984

Dick and Lois, my AA sponsors

My fifth husband, Mark P., on our wedding day, 1982

There are no pictures of Kushal T., my fourth husband.

Celebrating one year of sobriety with my friend, Marsha

My counseling center in Douglas, Wyoming

First reunion with Buffy and Shane, and Buffy's son, Jason, Oklahoma, 1985

First reunion with David, California, 1985

My sixth husband, Melvin, 1985

Rick W., my trucking partner, 1987

On the Sumrall television broadcast, 1987

My seventh husband, Mark H., 1988

Pastor Howard Jones, me, and his wife, Trish
TFC reunion, early 1990s

Pastor Jones helped with my deliverance in 1987

Living for Jesus!

The Women's Center, Hagerstown, MD, 1991

In Africa with Dr. Woo

Three weeks after my stroke at age 45, 1992

Me in 2010

COLLEGE

One day, Kirk, Amy, and Bob sat me down.

"You're wasting your life working for us," they told me. "Go train to be a counselor." Banner invested in me again, this time by paying part of my tuition to Minneapolis Community College (MCC). I earned an Associate's Degree in Chemical Dependency and Family Counseling, graduating in 1983.

Dr. Hastings, one of my professors, told me, "It doesn't matter how many degrees you get or how many books you read, Penny, you are a natural born counselor, so go by your guts." He wanted me to follow my intuition because I have an ability to see into people after I've spent some time with them.

Even without me, productivity at Banner continued to rise. They had a million-dollar month the quarter after I left. Part of their success was due to their engineering, and the other part was the way I boosted morale in the company.

During my MCC days, I went to work delivering newspapers. It was a job I loved, no matter how cold it was. It would be two or three o'clock in the morning, and there I would be delivering papers and talking to the Universe. I had a good route and, at Christmas time, made up to a thousand dollars in tips, candy, and cookies! The "Million Dollar Fudge" one of my customers made is still the best fudge I have ever eaten.

ON A LIZA NOTE...

I'm a Liza Minnelli look alike. In my earlier years, if I did my face and hair right, I could pass for her. Only my singing voice was different. During their childhood, when they went to a store where Liza was on a magazine cover, Shane would tell Buffy and David "That's what mom looks like."

Her life is parallel to mine. It's ironic, what she and I have been through.

When Liza Minnelli came to Minneapolis, I was

90

shopping in Dayton's store. When I went to check out, the manager said, "Oh, just sign your name Liza!"

I told them I wasn't Liza.

My friend knew one of her stage people and he told them about me. They thought I could be good publicity, so they dressed me like Liza and did my hair the way she had hers styled. During the concert, she came and stood in the audience and sang a song to me! It was exciting, and I didn't have to pay for my ticket either!

I follow her on Facebook. There are times when someone posts a picture of her and I feel like I'm looking at myself. Judy Garland was her mother.

Another artist who really influenced me was Janice Joplin.

It's interesting to look at Liza, Janice Joplin and myself – we were all in the occult. In both of them I see the rebel, the hippie, and the ladylike side of me. They did the same bouncing back and forth between these different personae.

Janice Joplin said, "They kicked me out of school, they kicked me out of town, and now I'm coming back as a star." When she died of an overdose of heroin, she had been clean for two years. For some reason, when she came home for a show she injected what someone gave her. It was too potent, and since she was clean, it was too much and she died. No one else sings the rock-n-roll blues like she did.

Janice Joplin taught me how to live that wild freedom and Liza Minnelli taught me how to be a lady.

DAD'S DEATH

During my tenure in Minneapolis, I met a Mormon named Mark P., who married me in 1982.

My dad passed away in 1983.

Mark and I went back to Wyoming for a visit before he died. My dad was really sick with a bad heart that had been getting worse for five or six years. He came with Mark and me and some friends to a picnic at Laramie Peak. When we tried to leave, our camper got stuck in a ditch. Sick as my dad was, unable to breathe, and barely able to move, he yelled at me to gun the engine and *lifted* that camper out of the ditch!

My dad needed a heart valve replaced. A few months later, I flew to the hospital in Denver to visit him. He was in the ICU and very weak, waiting for a pig valve to arrive from England. I sat with him the night before I had to fly back to Minneapolis. At 2:00 a.m., he sat up and talked to me. We forgave each other for everything. Then he lay back and slipped into a semi-coma. Two days later, my brother called to tell me he had died on the operating table. His last words were, "Let's get this show on the road."

Apparently, after the operation, his heart didn't start up again. The doctors came out to talk to my mom, who said to let him go if after thirty more minutes on the machine it didn't start again. It didn't. They let him go.

I flew in for the funeral that my brother planned. I will never get into another black limousine. My mom and brother couldn't get out of it for the funeral or the burial. There were hundreds of people at the gravesite and church. The pastor of the Mormon Church gave the eulogy and the military men folded the flag to give to me. They did a 21-gun salute because he was a veteran, but just before they shot, a whole herd of deer, my father's favorite animal, came and stood on the hill above the cemetery. The bucks, the does, the little fawns. They stood there, not moving through the whole 21-gun salute. They didn't move until the first shovelful of dirt hit my father's coffin. Then they turned and walked away, quietly.

Grampa Karspeck was there with me, and he and everyone else told me how strong I was. I thought, *Dad, you kicked me out of your life for your son, and that son is sitting in the car busted up. But here I am.*

92

MONEY

Two hours after the burial, the funeral home came and demanded three thousand dollars. I told them we would settle in the morning. My brother and I tried to figure out where we would get the money.

Suddenly, Mom said, "Daddy and I have a few cans of coins we can use." We went to the Converse Bank and it took them a week to count out the *thirty thousand dollars* in coins my parents had saved in three pound coffee cans! My brother put it in an account under my mom's name. I've never seen so many coffee cans full of coins in my life. My parents were from the Depression era, and they were worried they wouldn't have what they needed. Daddy was scared something would happen to him and Mom would have nothing. They didn't trust banks.

During Dad's hospitalization in Denver, I had been trying to get the Mormon Church to help with all the expenses because I assumed Mom was broke. Later, I found out she had had $1,500 with her the whole time!

She said, "You never asked me."

Mom lived on her Social Security check, but they cut it after Dad's death because she had that money in the bank under her name. My brother should have put it in his name, but he didn't realize why. She wasn't 65 years old yet. Daddy was 63 when he died and Mom would also be 63 when she died.

CHANGES

Jamey came back into my life at this time. He was ten years old and wanted to see me. We met, and he made the decision that he wanted to stay with me. When he called to tell his dad, CJ told him, "Fine, if that's what you want," and hung up on him.

I finished the internship associated with my AA degree from MCC and started "A New Day," an outpatient treatment center in Douglas, Wyoming. I ran it for about a year until President Reagan cut the funding.

I dealt with some volatile situations at A New Day. One I will never forget. The brother-in-law of one of my clients called me in a panic one night. He told me his sister-in-law, my client, was in danger. We drove over to her house where we found her husband standing over her with a 12-gauge shotgun up her vagina. I managed to talk him down, but I sure won't ever forget it!

In the meantime, Mark P. divorced me because he decided to have an affair with a lady he was home-teaching. I was upset about it. The Elders of the church told me it was my fault because I wasn't treating him right.

MELVIN

Melvin lived in Douglas, and I knew him from the bars in my pre-sober years. We started hanging out together. He told me he could take care of Jamey and me and had an oil pumper's job that paid 21 dollars an hour with good benefits. I didn't marry him for love, but for security. He was an okay guy. We tied the knot in Rapid City, South Dakota, where you could get married at the Justice of the Peace without a blood test.

When we got home, I found out that the house he said he could live in, his deceased parents' house, was actually his sister's. She didn't let us stay. His oil pumper's job was 21 dollars an hour, but only for two hours a week. He expected me to take care of him. We moved to a tent on the banks of the Platte River.

That winter, we went to work in the oil fields in northern Montana. Jamey stayed with my mom in Wyoming. I worked on the derrick, where I learned to throw the chain and pull the rod up out of the ground. For protection from the cold, we wore insulated coveralls that we had to buy. It was hard work, but the pay was good – you can make two to three thousand dollars a

94

week. In fact, my brother now owns five oil rigs.

Melvin and I traveled from Montana back to Douglas, Wyoming, after the job finished in the spring of 1985. There was nothing for us in Douglas, jobwise, and Jamey wanted to stay with my mom, so Melvin and I set out alone for the heat of Arizona and ended up in Albuquerque, New Mexico.

I thought it was a great opportunity to start a new clinic and a better life. I began as a waitress at the 76 Truck Stop in Albuquerque, but Melvin never got a job. I got sick of supporting him and told him so. He went back to Wyoming and divorced me.

I stayed true to my promises to God and didn't get back into drugs and prostitution. I rented an apartment, and Jamey, now 12 years old, came down to live with me for the summer and then went back to my mom's for school in the fall.

FULL CIRCLE

My first husband, Rick E., committed suicide on Good Friday in 1985. I had seen him the previous Labor Day. We had talked together, slept together, forgiven each other.

After his memorial service, the doors of the church blew open and the wind whistled through the building as they sang, "I Am Not here, Don't Cry for Me."

I drove my dad's pick-up home, coming down over the South Pass near Riverton, Wyoming, when the lights on the truck went out. I started praying, and I heard a voice, "It's okay, I'm here with you."

I looked over, and there in the passenger seat was Rick. He said, "I'll always be with you." The truck lights came on at the bottom of the canyon, but he was gone.

Precisely one year after Rick's death, mom's friend saw an ad in *The Douglas Budget* that said, "Buffy, Shane, and David are looking for their real mom. Call Buffy in Independence, Kansas." They had been ages four, three, and one when I last saw them.

Shane, Buffy, and I met in April 1985, at a McDonalds in Bartlesville, Oklahoma, where Shane was working as a manager. He was 22 years old. It was strange, because I didn't know them. Here were these grown people who were my kids, and I didn't know them. That's one of the strangest things. Even now, there is still no mother-child attachment there. I know I gave birth to them, but I didn't know them. I didn't raise them. In my mind, they were still four, three, and one.

We are not very close to this day.

In May, I went to meet David in Southern California, where he was stationed with the Army.

TWO STEPS BACK

In 1986, back in Albuquerque, I was raped by a customer at the 76 Truck Stop. Since I had to walk an hour across Albuquerque to get home after my shift at 10:00 p.m., I gladly accepted when a man offered me a ride. I didn't think anything of it until he turned off the road to my apartment and drove up the mountain. He grabbed me by my long hair and hit the power locks in his car. Today, I keep my hair very short and still flinch when I hear power locks click. He plea-bargained and got four years in the "sex farm" in Washington State, but I spiraled down into PTSD.

I ran away from Albuquerque.

RICK W.

Rick W. was a trucker I met in Albuquerque. He had visited my apartment, and after the rape, I flew to meet him in New York City. We trucked back across the country together and he dropped me off at my mom's in Douglas while he went to visit his wife and kids in North Dakota.

96

When I came to visit, I found that two doctors had come and taken Jamey out of my mom's house, charging her and me with being an unfit parent and grandparent.

Jamey was dating Dr. H's daughter. He met Dr. T. at a track meet. The two doctors were a general practitioner and a dentist who were involved with getting kids to do sexual stuff in exchange for money.

I went to court and had to fight against Dr. T. and his wife. It was election time, and I had my dad's six-shooter in my pants. My mom was petrified.

I told her, "Mom, I already lost three children. We are so poor they think they can take him away from us, too." I told her I would shoot my way out of there if I had to.

In my pocket were a pair of little red panties that Dr. T.'s wife had bought my son. I whipped them out and threw them at the judge.

"Tell me she doesn't have ulterior motives for wanting my son," I yelled. Then I turned to Dr. T., who was running for town-councilman in Douglas.

"Dr. T.," I said, "let me remind you that this is election year. If you take away my son, I will tell this story to every single radio station."

They dropped the case right there. They were buying my son with money and prestige, and Jamey ended up going along with them. He didn't speak to me for decades. When he got married, he claimed the dentist and his wife as his parents.

Jim Fagan, my attorney, said, "The rich buy poor people's kids everyday." Most trafficked kids are coming out of foster care, homelessness, or one-parent families. In those days they didn't call it human trafficking, but that's exactly what it was.

I don't know what happened or why he fell for all of it. Jamey said to me one time, "You really don't want to know what's happened." Now he's grown and has his own kids. I read his Facebook posts, and there are times when they are very dark.

END OF THE LINE

I can tell you, at this point I was not a nice person. Rick and I agreed that I would stay with my mom until he came and got me, but I was such a little maverick that I decided to go to him up in the little North Dakota town where he was with his family. My mom just shook her head. She had had enough of the way I was behaving.

She said, "Penny Kay, you are the devil himself."

I looked at her and laughed. "Oh, Mom, don't you know there's no such thing as the devil?"

Well, I took off walking and hitchhiking and showed up at Rick's in North Dakota. He just about had a fit, but he put me in the truck and we went off again. He got scared of me because, by now, I was a full-fledged witch, and all kinds of crazy things were happening. Several times, he woke up to find me with a knife to his throat ready to offer him as a blood sacrifice in the occult. We ended up at a 76 Truck Stop in Harrisburg, Pennsylvania, on July 13, 1987, where there was a mobile chapel sponsored and staffed by Transport for Christ (TFC), a Christian evangelism organization aimed at truckers.

JULY 13, 1987 - HARRISBURG, PENNSYLVANIA

At a truck stop, a trucker calls his company dispatcher and asks for a load. He receives an advance check to cover the expenses of going to pick it up, and away he goes. When he delivers, unloads, and returns to the terminal, he gets the remainder of the pay. We did not have a load when we pulled into the Harrisburg 76, totally broke, and we couldn't leave until we had an advance check.

Since Rick was a backslid Christian, he wanted to go in the chapel and ask for money and food, but I sure didn't. I told him to figure out a way to get some money so I could eat.

Rick headed for the chapel. He had seen Howard J., one

98

of the TFC ministers, there the last time we had stopped at this truck stop. I was in the convenience store when Howard told Melvin M., another minister with TFC, to find me and offer to buy me something to eat. I was hungry and angry, so I went with Melvin and Rick into the café and sat there talking to him so he would feed me.

As my blood sugar rose, my body was able to calm down and even out until I could hear Howard saying the same words Dick and Lois planted in me about a better life.

Did I believe it was going to work? That I could have this better life with Jesus?

No. I had been prayed over, baptized, and anointed before.

Did I want to play the game again?

Yes, if it would get me food and money.

While we ate, Pastor Al was on his way from Mechanicsburg. Then Melvin called the TFC prayer chain, the message went out, and people got into prayer for me.

Melvin and Pastor Al talked to me about this "better way." I played the game just to satisfy them so we could get money and food and keep going.

But that was not what happened, because God had something else in store for me. Once they took me to the upstairs room to pray over me, that's when the battle started between God and Satan. Pastor Al asked if they could do a deliverance, to ask God to send away the demons in me.

I didn't believe it would work. I had been through all kinds of stuff before in all kinds of churches with all kinds of people and nothing had changed. Way down deep inside me, though, was still that little girl with the purity of a newborn baby, the girl the angels spoke to. That purity was still in me, just waiting to be cracked open.

It was my time to get turned around.

DELIVERANCE

Pastor Al tells the story about the way he told everyone to leave the room if they didn't think they could handle hearing what would come out of my mouth when he started praying. He told them, "Your deepest, darkest sins are going to be revealed by the demons as they come out of her." When Melvin M. started fighting for me, we heard things from his childhood coming out of my mouth that were only known to him and God. He told me he felt for a minute like he would crumble, but then he remembered that God loved him and stood firm.

There were some people who wanted to be in the deliverance but left because they didn't want their secrets told.

We were in a room upstairs above the truck stop. The people down below in the cafe were suddenly faced with a choice while the fight was going on upstairs. Depending on where their souls were, some of them got up, got in their trucks and left. Others fell on their knees, prayed, and accepted Christ. I still get letters from people who contact me through Transport For Christ and tell me what was going on for them that day.

Pastor Al, through the power of the Holy Spirit, sent the demons out of me. Before they left, they slid my chair up the wall and held it there while they used my mouth to say all kinds of ugly things!

Melvin had a dark secret. His heart was not pure. That's why he could approach me without turning me off to his message about Jesus. When we were up there in that room, I told that secret of his. When he heard me, he gulped, but didn't stop the deliverance prayer.

When it was over, I was *so* different. I can remember that feeling to this day. It was two different women who walked in and out of there. Whoever the woman was that had lived my life up to that moment, died that day. The feeling inside now is totally, totally different. It's hard to put into words or even explain what it is like.

When Pastor Al did the deliverance, there were a

number of spirits that came out of me. He told me afterward that the Lord did not even let the last bunch be named. God told him to call them "Legion," and send them out in the name of Jesus, or they would destroy me.

I know the difference. I can *feel* the difference between how I felt before and how I felt after the demons left. Afterward, I didn't feel isolated anymore. Jesus was right there with me.

Now, I can tell when people are possessed. My spirit bears witness. They get really nasty with me. They hate me. They can't hurt me because I am covered by the Blood of Jesus Christ, the Holy Spirit is in me, and I am protected.

I was scheduled to offer myself as a blood sacrifice in August 1987. No one wanted me. No one cared about me. They just used me. So I figured I might as well be the next blood sacrifice. But God has a plan for each life, and in July 1987, Jesus stepped in and saved me.

That day, Jesus gave me the verse Hosea 4:6. "'My people are destroyed for lack of knowledge,'" he said. "I have enough preachers. I need a teacher. You."

POST-DELIVERANCE

After my deliverance and conversion, everyone involved went on a retreat. I got loved. People loved and cared about me. Doris was a member of the Church of the Brethren, and I was just me. I stayed with her. She sat on her bed, I sat on mine, and we talked about our lives – she, a wife and minister of the Brethren, me a witch. Her life was so clean, this clean family, and then there was me. We are still friends to this day.

I taught the TFC members as much as I could. This is why TFC is so relevant, so connected in fighting human trafficking. Now they know what I learned from being out there. Sometimes, I would explain a concept, and they would shake their heads and tell me I was lying. Then, a few months later, they'd say, "She told us about this, and look, here it is!"

In the beginning, I taught them about what was happening in the backs of those trucks and trailers that nobody saw. Then, God started bringing people into that mobile chapel that were coming out of all kinds of abusive situations. It was as if after their experience with me, God just opened up the doors.

My deliverance changed them. I still remember Howard J. He was a Baptist. He told me about the love of Jesus Christ. Later, he explained how my deliverance stretched everything he believed because his faith had been so boxed and so perfect. You must be a good person. You must study your Bible. You must pay your tithe. Yes, there is spiritual warfare, but it wasn't until after he met me that he came to understand what "spiritual warfare" means!

Sometimes, when life is hard, I go back and think on what it was like to feel so clean after being delivered and then I can continue on. It's like when you hear people say, "Go back to your first love [for Jesus Christ]." Remember what it was like on that first day when you gave your life to Christ. I go back and grab that feeling of, "Yes!" It's like the feeling of getting sober.

"I'm clean! I don't need coke! I don't need heroin!" It's like taking the hottest shower – you feel so clean.

During those times I question God, and life gets too hard, I go back to that moment when Christ reached down and grabbed me, and I knew I was clean of the drugs and alcohol.

That deliverance and my daily walk with Christ are the two most powerful forces in my life. That day made a big impression on a lot of people, especially me! I saw my deliverance through my eyes, they saw it through theirs, and what they saw was the power of God.

One thing I know and understand very well, now that I'm mature enough, is that if Christ had not cleaned me up and gotten me to a solid place, I would never have come through.

People ask why I didn't just get saved so I could be free of drugs and alcohol. Simply put, it doesn't work that way. I needed my body to be in good enough shape that I could hear the Holy Spirit talking to me. Then, I would be sure His voice was not just the hallucination from some drug I took.

When I was doing hallucinogenic drugs like LSD and PCP, I never got paranoid, but I went out into different worlds. If your body is not clean, your mind can't be strong and you have hallucinations from your blood sugar being messed up. If your blood sugar is messed up, you get wobbly and think you're hearing something that you're not. You can't tell the difference. You're in a semi-dream state.

MENTAL HEALTH AND THE SPIRITUAL

New technology and organizations like the City of Hope are looking at the spiritual realm as a part of mental health. They see it's not all chemical and physical. They see there is a spiritual side. We call them demons right in my classes in college. The new case teams include doctors, nurses, speech therapists, physical therapists, and people who know about the spiritual realm. A priest or a pastor is right there along with the medical and psychological staff because the traditional approach of medicine and counseling isn't working.

In a therapy setting, I talk about my occult experience, and patients talk about their Ouija boards and the things that come into their rooms at night.

To help support people coming out of the occult, you have to get close to them and be real. You have to have compassion and love for them. You have to do the action, not just say the words, or they won't listen to you. Howard J., the Transport for Christ chaplain on duty that day, never preached at me. He just showed compassionate care for me. There was no reinforcing of the old messages or that I had to do something. I had a choice. That's the key. If you can care compassionately, Christ will work right through you, but you have to be able to just care.

That's how it is for people coming out of human trafficking. You have to be able to do the actions for them, not just say words. They've heard it all, and they're not going to hear what you say. Instead, they're going to feel the feeling of you sitting on a dock with them kicking the water back and forth. Carefree timelessness is the basis of friendship. Friendship has to be in place before you can help.

Every child on this earth is God's child. No matter how bad their actions are. You have to get to that point where you can give that compassionate caring, if you're going to help the victims of human trafficking.

MY NEW LIFE

Immediately after my deliverance, we left the truck at the stop and went to a retreat in the Poconos Mountains. When we came back, Rick got a load and left.

He said, "I can't stay in your life. God has stuff for you to do and if I stay, I will be in your way."

Melvin M. put me on a plane and sent me to Casper, Wyoming, to talk to my mom. She wouldn't come to the airport to get me because she didn't believe I had really changed. My sister, Patty, and brother-in-law, Tom, picked me up. When I walked through the door of my mother's house, she looked at me.

"Penny Kay, you've met Jesus," she said simply.

"Yes, Mom, I have," I said. I knew if my mom could tell, it must be true.

While I was in Douglas, I got my occult stuff out of the attic of my great-granddad's house and burned it in a barrel during the daytime. Then I flew to South Bend, Indiana, to attend Dr. Lester Sumrall's World Harvest Bible College. The Mennonite congregation that Melvin M. belonged to sent me there because Melvin M.'s daughter, Susan, lived in South Bend. She thought I would be best understood if I went to the school, as Dr. Sumrall had written books about deliverance. He was known as a person who could put your testimony on worldwide television. And he did. He sold book after book, and my television segment was viewed many, many times.

Sister Sumrall, the wife of Dr. Sumrall, prophesied over me in the parking lot and told me that a day would come when I would stand before kings, queens, presidents, senators, and counselors, and that I would proclaim Jesus Christ as the King.

HUSBAND NUMBER SEVEN

In late 1987, I was working at a job I loved in South Bend, Indiana, at LaHayre's Dress department store, when Mark H. came into my life. He was a nice Christian guy who treated me like a little queen...until we got married on January 14, 1988.

I remember the disoriented feeling of getting married and then saying, "What just happened?" It was like, how did I get married? I just never expected I would do it. It was like I was in this fog and ended up in a marriage.

Soon, I discovered Mark was mentally ill. He had been married previously, but it had not worked out. His family was tired of dealing with him, so they were happy I came along. Before long, his disease progressed to the point where he would hide in the closet when our friends came to visit. He was afraid I would kill him because I had come out of the occult.

My first paid speaking engagement came soon after we married. I was given fifteen hundred dollars in donations, and Mark promptly quit his job.

My mom sent Jamey, now seventeen, out to live with me.

"Mark is nuts," Jamey said. "He's going to kill you before this is over, and I don't want to be here when he does. I'm going back to Grandma"

I thought, *Jamey, you're crazy.*

When I talked to a psychiatrist, however, he told me Mark was a paranoid schizophrenic and warned me that I could end up dead because he was so dangerous.

CHOOSE YOU THIS DAY

Melvin M., who had helped in my deliverance, didn't believe in divorce but he told me not to refuse if Mark asked to divorce me. A speaking engagement in Hagerstown, Maryland, called me out of South Bend. On the way out of the city, God spoke to me. He told me to choose between Him and Mark. I was to keep driving if God was to be the center of my life, or turn around and go home if it was going to be Mark.

"Lord, I will follow you," I said, and kept driving. That event in Maryland kicked off my speaking career, and for the next six years I ran up and down the East Coast speaking about my conversion. I had a small office in Keyser, West Virginia, which I ended up closing because I was always on the road.

I got my divorce papers from Mark in 1990 and haven't dated since. I asked God to remove all that from me, and he did, so I don't get caught up in that whole dating/marriage scene.

ON THE SPEAKING CIRCUIT

I remember speaking in Cumberland, Maryland, at the Boys' Club. The incarcerated teens were telling me how powerful Satan is, and I was telling them how powerful Jesus is. They didn't believe me, so I asked them, "Okay, if Satan is so powerful, how come you're still in jail and I'm free?" Some of those boys still send me Christmas cards.

The first time I spoke at the Venice Inn in Florida, there were 650 people there, including all kinds of police officers who wanted to hear me talk about coming out of the occult world. There were three or four Satanists sitting there, and a few years later, they contacted TFC to say they gave their lives to Jesus because of hearing me.

106

At a talk in Bowling Green, I told the organizers, "The witches are coming around the corner."

They looked at me uneasily.

"They're here," I said, and in they walked. They were dressed in their robes and sat right in the front row.

The organizers said, "What are we going to do?"

"Just pray," I said. "You're going to see the power of Jesus."

I turned my back to them and begged Jesus to come and help me. The witches sat so still through the whole presentation, the whole prayer, the whole invitation, it was as if they were frozen. They couldn't move. The power of God held them down in their chairs.

The week before in the same room, a practicing witch came to talk and very few came to hear. At my talk, it was standing room only. The only thing the witches were able to do was write on the comment card, "She's crazy." All Jesus let them do was sit there and stare at me.

It was a really great witness to the young people there.

God took me to Tampa to teach spiritual warfare to a youth group that wanted to break up a big, famous evil parade held there each year - a night of really bad stuff. I told the youth, "If you are not strong in your Christian walk, don't go." Some of them stayed home. I told them to use the buddy system, because it's a jungle down there. We locked arms and walked the parade singing, "You Will Know We Are Christians By Our Love." Then we got in our vans and went home.

The next year, the parade was cancelled.

A gentleman from the Fellowship of Christian Athletes heard me speak somewhere and invited me to give a talk at the Naval Academy in Annapolis, Maryland. I ended up speaking there twice.

Not everything is perfect when you're speaking at churches.

Churches would bring me in, make up a whole advertising campaign, take in a huge offering at my talk, and only give me one-quarter of it. One pastor saw this happening and told me not to let them prostitute me.

God told me not to ask for any money, but that he would provide for me.

When you're speaking in a home setting, the money part is not an issue, since they don't take an offering, but usually someone will give me enough money to cover my expenses.

The other part of public speaking is the way people use you for their own causes. Even today, people try to latch on to me and my story to get publicity for their own causes.

MOM'S DEATH

Mother died in January 1989. I didn't go home for the funeral because my brother was there and I had just been there for a Christmas visit. She is buried in Douglas right next to my daddy. She had three wishes before breast cancer took her life. She asked God not to give her a lot of pain, not to let her die by herself, and please to save her daughter, Penny Kay.

Dr. Johnson said she didn't have as much pain as some do. At the end, her two good friends walked into the hospital to visit her. She lifted up her head, smiled at them, and died. And here I am today. God answered all her prayers.

Keeping secrets killed her. She didn't tell anyone about her breast cancer until it had broken through the skin of her breast and she was in agony. When she sent Jamey to South Bend, I called her and asked what was going on. That's when I learned what she had been hiding from everyone. It was December 1987. The coming April, she had a mastectomy. The next month, on my birthday, the other breast was removed. In January, she died. She had a lump the size of a small grapefruit when I walked in, and it was horrible looking.

"How could you *not* know it was cancer?" I cried.

Dr. Johnson, her doctor, told me she willed herself dead. He said, "When people choose to die, they die." Her body was fighting to stay alive, but she had already left. I understand why, what with Dad gone.

When I came home at Christmas, she hadn't eaten for days.

"They're starving me to death," she told me.

"Why aren't they feeding her?" I asked my sister.

"She doesn't eat what they bring her," my sister replied.

"You're not dealing with your mother, you're dealing with cancer," Dr. Johnson told me, "and that is a spirit all its own."

During my visit, I cooked for her and she ate and ate.

"Don't hold on to me," she wheezed one night, lying on the couch. I sat nearby watching her breathe, counting her exhalations. "Don't pray to keep me here. Let me go."

"I ain't praying for that Mom," I told her. "I'm just praying you don't have a lot of pain."

My little sister said mom quit eating as soon as I left. She was only maintaining because I was there. She died a week later and I didn't feel guilty. I knew she was ready to go.

My brother has never, never gone back to my great-granddad's property in Douglas, Wyoming, where my mother was living in her little travel trailer. Even though my sister lives on the property now, he waits out on the road in the car. The memories are too strong.

BRAKES

Mark H. divorced me in 1990, the same year I started The Women's Center in Hagerstown, Maryland, to minister to women who had been abused or were in difficult relationships.

That year, I went on a mission trip to Mexico, and the next year, to Africa. I went with an 80-year-old woman on an ophthalmology project. We went to Lagos, Nigeria, and 300 miles north into the jungle.

Prior to a trip to Ecuador in 1993, I decided to visit my

son, David, in Florida, then Buffy in Kansas, and Shane in Arizona. Providentially, I had closed The Women's Center before leaving, because, as soon as I arrived in Florida, I had a stroke. I lay in the hospital, unable to move.

I thought God was telling me I needed to keep letting go of the world, and to keep letting go of wanting people's approval.

The hospital treated me well. I was there for twenty-four hours without even being able to blink my eyes. After a week, I was discharged and went to David's. There was so much turmoil there I called Liz and Woody Atwood and asked if I could come recuperate at their house in Hancock, Maryland. My friends, the Jennings, from North Myrtle Beach, came and drove me and my car to their house. I wasn't allowed to drive, and I really couldn't. Still, I only stayed overnight with the Jennings and took off the next day for Maryland. I could only drive for a while, and then I had to pull over because my eye would not shut. It felt like sand, staring into the bright sun. I finally got to Hancock and stayed with the Atwood's for six months. Liz had been a client at The Women's Center and we were best friends.

I couldn't go out into the sunshine because my pupil would not dilate and the eye could not water. I had to wear sunglasses even at night. When I walked, I dragged my foot.

Finally, I was well enough to live on my own. My friends gave me their old camper, which I was allowed to park on the land of some other friends.

ON THE RUN

I started at Shepherd College in Shepherdstown, West Virginia, in 1995, studying for a Bachelor's of Psychology. I was the talk of the school because I decided to run for governor of West Virginia. Some of the students were behind me, but when it came right down to it, they walked away because it conflicted with the politics of their parents.

110

While I was running for governor, I lived in the woods. The press took pictures of me with my car trunk full of clothes to send to the Indian reservation in South Dakota. Jay Leno and David Letterman heard that I had come out of the occult world and said, "What do you expect from West Virginia?"

A friend from South Carolina saw me in Star Magazine at a Wal-Mart in his hometown. He called to tell me, and I went down to buy a copy. Sure enough, there I was on page two, big as life next to the trunk filled with clothes.

I was talked about everywhere. Then, I spent thousands of dollars on a campaign event in Morgantown, West Virginia, and no one showed up. My ambitions came crashing down around me.

"What the heck?" I said to myself. I told God goodbye and drove my car down the boat ramp into the Potomac River. A fisherman came by and pulled me out. He took me to East Ridge in Martinsburg, a mental health unit.

I met Dr. Shapiro at East Ridge. He diagnosed me with bipolar disorder and said I had it all my life. The doctor thought the stress must have brought on this episode that ended with me driving into the river, but other events in my life were likely a result of the imbalance, too. Things I didn't even remember, as I had been so manic at the time.

Dr. Shapiro told me there was no reason for me *not* to kill myself, considering what I had been through. Once he gave me permission to commit suicide, sure enough, I started fighting to live.

He taught me how to chart my moods and cycles. I know when I'm high and when I'm low, and I know what to do when I'm in between. If I'm making a decision, I ask myself if it is my bipolar or me. If it's a big decision, I force myself to wait twenty-four hours so impulsiveness doesn't get the better of me. I also talk about it. I tell the secrets. When I'm feeling antsy and have the urge to run off, I talk about it so the urge can't become a monster.

"What is the reason you wanted to run for governor?"

111

Dr. Shapiro asked. "I certainly wouldn't want to be governor!"

I looked at him and asked him what he was talking about. I had been so manic during that time I didn't even remember running. I had not done any drugs or alcohol, but I was just chemically imbalanced. I took bipolar medication for five years and learned to watch my patterns.

I don't take it lightly, but he taught me not to be ashamed of my mental illness. I don't ever go as high on my manic stages now as I did then. It has become a joke. I'll tell people, "I'm a little manic, but I'm not going to run for governor."

Even government officials have now come out and spoken about their alcohol, drugs, and bipolar. The three weave together, although not all bipolar people are alcoholic.

When you get into alcohol, drugs, the occult, it all melds together. It's a bizarre kind of world. Dr. Shapiro didn't want me to feel like less of a person because I have bipolar disorder, though. He gave me Patty Duke's book, *Brilliant Madness*. Ted Turner is also bipolar. When someone is manic and working for a company that understands them, the company will use the employee's manic-ness and pay them well for it, because in that state your creative brain is really busy.

Ted Turner has a group around him that brainstorms with him when he gets manic. When he's down, they hold on to him, love him, and care for him.

There is more and more push to understand mental heath, but I found that people with a mental illness are more likely to get into the occult world because of the labels and stigma of the "regular" world. In the occult world, they're accepted.

Now, society is changing. The Western world still stigmatizes and locks away mentally ill people where other cultures hold, take care of, and learn from them. They believe it is a gift.

SUICIDE ATTEMPTS

In the year 1955, I witnessed two suicides. I was eight years old.

One guy shot himself in the field and one in his bathroom. I helped my dad clean up. One was my dad's friend, and the other I saw because my dad was helping and I helped him. I'm not sure of the effect it had on me; I disassociated with it. But it is true that when things in my life got despairing, I tried suicide, too, simply because all my troubles would be over in a minute, like for those men.

Now that I have been diagnosed, I understand why suicide was so much a part of my life and why it ran in my family. It is a prominent symptom of bipolar disorder, which is hereditary.

I first attempted suicide when I was nine years old, because who cared about me? My dad didn't. The one who used to call me his "little man" and have me follow him all around helping him, had a son now. My mother's only interests were her *True Story* magazines, drinking coffee, and smoking cigarettes.

So, I took a razor blade and cut horizontally. Of course, it didn't work. I got my behind spanked, and dad bandaged up my wrists. In those days, there were no counselors to take me to and no money for a psychologist, so I didn't get any help.

My second attempt came when I was eleven, after the City Councilman in Glen Rock molested me. In order to pet his horses, I had to go in the cornfield with him. I took a whole bottle of aspirin, but the only effect was vomiting and diarrhea.

When I was about fourteen, I tried for the third time. Three times I tried to shoot myself with a .30-30, but it would not fire unless it was pointed away from me.

After I married Rick E., I tried to commit suicide again. This time I took pills. Virginia, Rick's mother, slapped me across the face.

"What do you think you're doing, Penny?" she yelled.

113

"Grow up!"

As my life continued, I was doing so many drugs that it was like a constant suicide attempt. In Minneapolis, I went out and bought a brand new Lariat rope and was going to hang myself. My husband, Mark P., had gone off with a lady he was home-teaching in the Mormon Church. I was in the middle of an affair, and was hopeless. I went downstairs and strung myself up, kicked the chair from underneath me, and the rope broke! A brand new Lariat! I was so mad, I returned the rope and got my money back. The guy at the store couldn't believe it. He said, "These things don't break!"

After that, my attitude was, "What the heck? Nothing works!"

The final time I tried to commit suicide was when I ran my car into the Potomac River after everything fell apart in my run for governor.

When I sat in AA meetings, though, I realized my suicide attempts weren't any different from anyone else's. In AA, we sit around and say, "We have a purpose! We are still alive!" For some of them, the gun went off, but it only shattered things. Some of them spent months in the hospital, but they're still here. God has a purpose for each life.

I survived, too. I'm still surviving.

A HOUSE ON THE MOUNTAIN

In 1996, I was in treatment with Dr. Shapiro and living in the camper. In treatment, I met Sue, who owned a house in a community on the side of a mountain in Gerrardstown, West Virginia. She had lots of good things to say about living there.

On the day I was supposed to go to closing for a little house in the development, I was begging God for help. I had no money. Not a dime. In an hour's time, I was supposed to show up at the title company with three hundred dollars. How in the world was God going to work this one out? I walked over to the post office and checked the mail, still talking to God. In my mailbox was a letter from a friend and in it, a check for three hundred dollars! God has always helped me at the last moment!

I bought the house, hidden down off the side of the mountain above a creek. Later, I didn't have the money to pay the bills. I had used the money to help a single mom make her car payment. Now she is the manager of one of the radio stations here. She is remarried and has another child and is really grateful for the help that kept her off the streets with her little girl. To take care of her, I lived there for years without water or electricity.

After I had been living on the mountain for a year, I went to work at Shoney's restaurant in Martinsburg, West Virginia, as a food bar attendant and at Sheetz as a cashier. When my car broke down, I had to walk eleven miles each way to work. I had to leave my house at midnight to be there to open the store at 5:00 a.m. The car broke five times that summer.

In the kitchen of the Shoney's restaurant where I worked, there were two great big kettles separated by a sink and a sprayer. Since I had no water or electricity on the mountain, I would stand in there and take a shower and wash my clothes through the dishwasher when everyone else had gone home!

During all of this, I managed to keep up my studies. In the spring of 2000, I graduated from Shepherd College with a Bachelor's degree in Psychology firmly in hand.

YOUTH LEADER

I must have been born with it.

All through my life, I was always influencing and guiding young people. At first, I led them into trouble. Look at the kids who were willing to follow me into stealing cars and writing bad checks! Now, and when I worked in restaurants, I teach young people ethics. I volunteer to do extra cleaning in order to teach them by example. I teach them how to have

115

integrity, how not to cheat, how to speak politely, and to treat one another with respect.

I am also very open about Jesus Christ, who is stronger than their friends. Today, the kids who worked for me are managers, they have families, they are in church, and it's because of that example. It's not that I'm special, it's that God wants me to teach the youth. Something I have come to understand is that I am a spiritual leader. I've known it all along, but I am really beginning to recognize how I can use it in the holistic treatment of human trafficking victims.

When I was the night manager at Shoney's restaurant, it was my first Friday Night Seafood Bar when all of a sudden I realized half of my cooks and servers were gone.

I grabbed the sleeve of one of the older servers. "Where'd everybody go?"

She jerked her chin toward the back door. I pushed open the sagging screen and peered out into the employee parking lot. There was no one to be seen, but several cars were swaying, their windows foggy.

I marched up and knocked on the window of the closest car. "Excuse me," I called through the window, "there's a customer who needs some coffee." In a couple of minutes, the cooks and servers shambled inside, red-faced.

"Wash your hands and get busy," I told them. That's when I became a real manager. The kids respected me for my forthrightness.

Raymond, the cook, used to kneel and tie my shoes for me. Now he is the bookkeeper for an ice company. Every once in a while we'll talk about his kindness, and he says he would do it again for me.

When I went on a medical mission trip to Africa, I met another person who works with youth the way I do. I was assigned to work with a dentist from China, Dr. Woo. He actually taught me how to pull teeth, not just how to hand him instruments.

Dr. Woo said in his country they teach skills to as many

116

people as possible so the society can move forward. That's not how it is in Western countries where the medical professionals are afraid you will learn the skills and take their jobs. When I'm teaching management to youth, I teach like Dr. Woo. I teach them how to take over my job.

A NEW HIP

About the time of my graduation from Shepherd, my hip started to hurt. I thought the ache was curable with Ibuprofen, but in the summer, I went to the doctor.

"You need a hip replacement," Dr. Cincinnati said, turning from the x-ray. "See the crack in the bone here? A nerve is down inside that crack, and that's why the pain is so intense."

"No surgery," I objected, "God will heal me."

"God uses doctors as an extension of his hands, so you might need a surgeon to help you heal," he insisted.

Still I refused.

He folded his hands on top of my chart. "You'll be back when the pain gets bad enough."

I left the office and told God I would give up chocolate for six months, if only he would heal me.

I worked 12 to 14 hours every day for a year on that broken hip, and it only got worse. The pain was so bad I ate two bottles of Advil a day just to keep it manageable. Some of the days the pain was so bad I couldn't carry my purse or a pan of mashed potatoes from the kitchen to the hot bar at Shoney's.

The cleaning that used to take an hour after closing now took me all night. Often, I would finish and leave ten minutes before the morning-shift arrived. I was in horrible pain and would cry all night.

As the pain grew, I started to find pennies. I knew God was with me because I would find pennies in the most unusual places, and they reminded me that God was thinking of Penny.

After closing time, I had to scrub the floors in the

kitchen, vacuum the floor, and clean the hot bar. Sometimes God and the angels came to help me clean the restaurant.

Once, I limped to the bathroom, begging for a sign that God was there with me. A sign I couldn't miss. I was crying with pain as I eased into the bathroom stall. There was a penny on the toilet set. From that time on, I'd find pennies by the grill, or on the cabinet, wherever I was. The pennies showed up outside the restaurant, too. The parking lot, in my driveway. To this day, when things are hard, I still find pennies in odd places.

I was able to sit down, but walking was nearly impossible, and I certainly couldn't carry anything. Not even my purse. Just that small weight hurt me so much. I would go to the grocery store and honk my horn until an employee came out, got my money, and bought my cat and dog food for me.

When I did make it home and parked, I had to crawl down the driveway on my belly, the pain was so bad.

One night at 3:00 a.m., as I was crawling down the hill, I started screaming at Jesus.

"You're just like every other man! You just use me, beat me, and leave me!" On and on I ranted at him, gravel tearing the skin on my stomach and excruciating pain in my hip.

Instantly, I was standing upright on my deck in front of my door. I was just – there. I knew it was Jesus and the angels that had lifted me off my belly and set me down by the door. In shame and gratitude, I began to cry.

In January 2002, I was back in Dr. Cincinnati's office.

"Is the pain bad enough?" he asked, raising his brow.

I said, "Let's go to surgery." He was ready to operate the next day, but I insisted we wait until February so my work replacement would be back from her own surgery.

During that year of pain, my house was a wreck. I was just surviving, and I hurt so badly I couldn't clean it. On the way to the hospital, I had to call my friend Debbie to come and carry my suitcase and my dog to the car because I couldn't. I asked her to clean my place and not tell anyone how bad it was.

When I got to the house where my dog was going to

board, my friend came running out of the house and up to the car. She grabbed me and said, "You don't have to be strong any more. We are going to take care of you." It was such a relief to hear those words!

Tara, my cocker spaniel, had not been brushed once during the whole year of pain. My friends had her groomed and trimmed while I was in the hospital.

When they took me to the hospital, the nurse settled me into bed and echoed the words of my friend, "Penny, you don't have to be strong anymore."

Dr. Cincinnati operated the next morning, and for the first time in two years, I woke up with no pain. Afterwards, the surgeon told me that when he opened me up, he used a scoop to take out my hip. It had completely decayed inside me because I had waited so long.

Besides being an excellent orthopedic surgeon, Dr. Cincinnati is a cute-looking guy! Everyone I send to him tells me, "Oh, yes! You're right! He is a cutie!" A faithful Catholic, Dr. Cincinnati told me, "There's more going on in surgery than just the fixing of your hip!" I know he was praying for me. Later, I followed him into the Catholic Church.

Two months of rehab later, I went back to work at the restaurant. Later that year, the friend who took care of my dog and told me I didn't have to be strong, got sick. She didn't know she had ovarian cancer until it was too late, and she died in agony. Although I rubbed her aching muscles, I couldn't take away her pain like she did for me.

CRASH

On June 1, 2008, I had just retired after twelve years at Shoney's, and was driving down a rainy Route 11 in West Virginia. My mind was busy. I was talking to God about the friends I was about to visit, the day-old bread I was about to pick up, and how we were going to manage to pay for the car repairs that were reaching the critical stage.

Suddenly, a pick-up truck came up from the side and hit me square in the driver's side door. I slammed on the brakes, driving the metal rod in my hip into the bone, shattering it.

The other driver bounced out of the T-bone and hit me again. He was an 81-year-old man with his wife in the passenger seat, and he didn't even realize he hit me. They were both uninjured, although his wife had some scratches from the safety glass.

When I got out of the car, it hurt, but I didn't realize the impact damaged my hip.

"I didn't see you!" he kept saying.

The ambulance arrived, and I let them check me out. Dr. Cincinnati taught me how to wiggle my butt to check for pain or sounds that shouldn't be there. There were neither, so I thought I was okay and chose not to go to the hospital.

The next day, I went to my chiropractor, who took an x-ray. It was easy to see the broken screws in my new hip. He told me to go see Dr. Cincinnati and sent the x-rays over. I waited for the office to call me with an appointment, but they didn't.

Meanwhile, I walked on the hip and started hurting worse and worse until I could hardly stand, but still no call from the doctor's office. Finally, I called them myself and said, "Didn't you get the x-rays or the message? I really need to see Dr. Cincinnati! I can hardly walk!" They found the message in a stack of unread mail.

In a flash, I saw the doctor, who surgically repaired my hip and went on vacation while I went to rehab for the second time, healing beautifully.

Then one night, in the middle of rehab, I settled down in my bed to eat a cup of Jell-O. Out of habit, I wiggled my hip to check for pain or sounds. Something happened. The next morning, they came and walked me to rehab, commenting on the pain noises I was making. I made them all through my physical therapy session and all the way back to my room. Suddenly, the room was full of people sticking needles in my

120

hand. The doctor on duty came in and said, "I hate to be the bearer of bad news, but the hip fell apart."

Dr. Cincinnati came back from vacation just before the doctor on duty took me in for surgery. When he looked at the x-rays, he saw my hipbone crumbled in pieces. The accident had cracked the bone, and rehab shattered it into slivers. Instead, he sent me to a specialist, who told me to put my affairs in order because the more-intense and invasive operation he was about to perform on me has only a 50 percent survival rate.

Off to surgery I went for the second time, only to be stopped mid-procedure for lack of blood. My blood is very rare, and I waited three weeks before enough was found to continue. Before the third surgery, the doctor refused to see me in the operating room unless enough blood was in there first.

Finally, the blood arrived, the surgery happened, and I completed rehab. They cut the same scar four times, and now, I have a dimple in my bottom! The hospital had a bone bank, and thank goodness they were able to match my bone instead of having to scrape one of my own for material for the bone graft.

I went home on November 23. The insurance of the man who hit me covered all the medical bills, and I go in for a check-up once a year. My hip is a mass of metal. It has screws, a long rod, a block, clamps, and wires, which the doctor said he tried to tie into bows for me.

GRADUATE SCHOOL

While my hip was healing, I did a lot of sitting around. There wasn't much I *could* do. At the time, Brenda and Jessica, a homeless mother and her adult daughter, were living with me. Jessica was going to school to be a mortician. Brenda wanted to go to school to be a medical technician. As I was helping them get their degrees, I saw an ad on the Internet for a distance learning university. Because they were kind and didn't make me feel dumb for not having much experience with a computer, I decided to enroll in a Master's of Business degree program in November of 2010.

Brenda and I did homework together – we'd help each other. One night, I was doing research when I noticed an advertisement from the Polaris Project in the sidebar of my computer. It was about helping the victims of human trafficking. I clicked on the link, and something clicked inside of me. I realized several things:

- o I had been sold as a sex slave, just like these women Polaris was trying to help.
- o I had a great experience at a halfway house after the hospital in Minneapolis.
- o I craved the community experience of the commune and the camaraderie I experienced in the occult world.
- o I loved farming and ranching.

How cool if I could have a farm where women could come and heal like I did, I thought. *It would be called 'Coffeehouse Farm,' because it would be a casual, inviting place where people could come. A place you'd like to sit down with a cup of coffee and talk. A place where there are horses to help women move forward.* I knew I wanted to be a part of the effort to help victims of human trafficking.

When I made the decision to help, I chose a new direction for my study. Once I was done with the MBA, I went back to get a Master's in Psychology so I could be an Applied Behavioral Analyst, and make treatment plans for these women.

It's these little occurrences that make you realize how God is pushing you toward something. It's these little signs that are so easy to overlook that make you see a new path that God wants you to follow.

In November 2011, I decided to sell everything, move off the mountain, and get involved in helping victims of human trafficking.

THE WALK

Another "God nudge" came when a friend and I were talking about the history of Route 11, an historic byway through the Shenandoah Valley in Virginia.

"It was originally the Indian road," she told me.

The Indian road, I thought, images of my great-grandmother rising in my mind. The warrior path. And suddenly, I knew.

"I'm going to walk Route 11," I announced. "It will be a walk to raise awareness for human trafficking, because the road parallels Interstate 81, a major corridor for tractor-trailer based human trafficking.

I started out on a hot summer day in July 2014, in the parking lot of Old Court House Square in Martinsburg, West Virginia. Over the next few weeks, I walked sections of Route 11 until I arrived nearly two hundred miles to the south at Natural Bridge, Virginia on August 18. The awareness raising began almost immediately since my safety vest was emblazoned with the words, "Stop Human Trafficking."

I was walking down the street in Martinsburg, West Virginia, and decided to go into Dominos for a bottle of cold water. A girl came in with a guy, and they ordered something in a bag and walked out. I drank my water, talked with the clerks, and left. A block and a half later, between two hotels, there was the girl sitting on a rock eating her lunch. I went over and talked to her and handed her my card. We talked about everyday stuff and the better way of life.

Suddenly, a voice behind me told me to stop talking. I turned around and saw a man with a knife on his belt that gestured at me to keep on moving. As I was walking away, a pickup truck turned into the hotel. She got up and got into the truck, and it was very evident that the guy in the truck had bought her. She's still there. I see her every once in awhile. I've called the hotline, and the cops are up and down there all the time. I'm just waiting for them to get caught. There are fifty-two prostitutes in the area now, all of them strung out on heroin.

A reporter wrote about my Walk in an article that was picked up by the Associated Press. Two readers from New York City with ties to a human trafficking victim came forward and offered to purchase a farm where I could establish a refuge for young women newly freed from slavery.

THE POWER OF SEX

I was six years old when I was raped on the school ground. At nine, it was the City Councilman in Glen Rock. At thirteen, I was gang-raped at a party in Glen Rock. From that point on, I was raped, molested, and prostituted throughout my life. There were more than a hundred separate episodes.

Once, my mom and dad gave me some money to go out with friends. I was driving, and I stopped for beer. We got drunk, and I passed out. When I woke up, they had raped me, taken my money, and left me broke on a country road.

My whole life was about sex. Every month, in one way or another, someone would use me. When I was in school, teachers had sex with me in the bathroom. There was always someone, all the time. It got to the point where I didn't think I was good for anything else.

After I was saved in 1987 and divorced Mark H., it was the end of sex for me. No more. Such freedom! I never had to do that again, or have anybody touch me again! Finally, it was *my* body.

I told myself, "I *choose* this body, and no one has permission to touch it!" And no, I don't miss sex!

I was given some very mixed messages as a child. When I stood in front of the judge at age six and listened to him tell me I was a bad little girl, it was a lie, but it made a mess of many years of my life. I always wondered if people treated me as nothing more than a sex object because I had acne. Or was it because I wanted to be cared about? But to Rick E., my

124

husband, the father of my children, I was nothing more than something he could sell to get money for his booze. Or to Jim H., I was just something that could be traded to the landlord for rent, so he could spend his money on heroin instead of housing.

What I needed was to be loved for who I was, not for my body.

Drinking and drugging filled that love-need for a while, but I had an underlying anger that never went away. I would pick up these guys, take them to bed, get up and say 'Thanks and bye.'

They'd say, "Can I call you?"

I'd say, "Why?"

It didn't help that I was doing Ouija Boards and chants. Now, through physics, I understand that you have to invite Christ into your life. It's the same with the devil. He has to be invited in.

Another strike against me was that we lived on the wrong side of the tracks. The message that I was not good for anything but sex was hammered into me. If you want acceptance, the price is sex.

Tom L., the blond-haired, blue-eyed basketball player helped reinforce the message. I asked him to take me to the dance. I earned new Bobby socks by working really hard. After waiting and waiting, it was finally nine o'clock, and I walked to the school.

"Hi, Tom," I said, coming up to where he was standing with the Reid twins. He took one look at me and turned away. I didn't know what to do.

"We were going to meet at 9:00," I reminded him. The Reid girls laughed.

He turned around and reinforced the reason for my existence.

"I'd meet you in the back of a car," he scoffed, "but not at a school dance!"

After that, I hung it up at school.

Even after treatment, this message continued to be reinforced. When I was in my internship at MCC, Loren, my counselor, broke every client/counselor rule there was. He finally ended up living at my house for a while until he got his own place. Looking back at that chapter in my life, I'm just disgusted. But that's what he did.

And so, in 1986, when I was brutally raped in Albuquerque, I called my mother and told her what had happened to me. That was when I found out about her rape at sixteen. She told me to come home and not tell anyone. I refused both requests. I was done being a victim.

The man raped me in October, and the court date wasn't until April. During the interim, he was not allowed to come near me or the truck stop where I was working, but that didn't stop his friends from threatening me. That's the reason many rape victims never tell. It's hard enough to prove that you weren't selling sex or trying to get them to have sex with you. On top of that, you're dealing with all the emotions of being raped. If you add the pressure of his friends harassing you, you'll drop the charges unless you are very strong.

I did not drop the charges. But when the legal battle was over, I had a bad PTSD episode and ended up trucking with Rick W. as his sex partner.

The ladies coming out of human trafficking are in a similar situation. These ladies are doing fifteen to twenty guys a day. I used to think getting someone out of the occult was really, really hard, but it's worse when you're dealing with human trafficking. These women have so much more to deal with: abortion, drugs, prostitution, selling their babies if they get pregnant.

It's crucial to train the women coming out of human trafficking to *do* something. That's why horses are so important. They give the women something to do, something to focus on. Horses are also healing animals, so they are helping heal the women at the same time.

I remember the time in Florida that Jamey and I went to the beach. We talked to people and goofed off all afternoon, having a good time. Some guy asked where I lived, and I told him. Jamey and I went back to the house that afternoon. I fed him and was starting to get settled down when there was a knock at the door. It was the guys from the beach. They held a gun to Jamey's head and raped me, saying they would kill him if I told anyone.

Who are you going to tell, if you're doing drugs?

You can't imagine what I've lived through.

What I do now is the way to break this cycle of sexual abuse.

When I went to Big Piney to visit my granddaughter, I was pushing her on the swing and told her, "It stops here. Grandma's going to make sure the sexual abuse in our family stops here." Yes, my family members all have problems, but no one is being sexually abused. I said it wasn't going to happen anymore and I stopped that negative energy.

That's why I am so passionate about the farm I'm starting to help ladies coming out of human trafficking. That's why I feel so strongly about leaving this footprint. People may not understand, but I am simply giving back when I guide and help and do this for another human being.

It's not just being sad about what happened, it's what you do about it. Are you stopping the damage or are you feeding it?

There is one question I have. A question I'm always trying to answer: *What drives men so mad that they have to have this sex, no matter the cost to another human being?*

What?

It applies to all men. The women who are trafficking girls are doing it because they themselves were hurt so badly, but the majority of the traffickers, at least ninety percent, are men.

All of them consumed with making money and having sex.

GOD IN MY LIFE

Every time God is about to move in my life, a man

comes along and tempts me with all the creature comforts I don't have. That's when I know something big is on the way.

Once, it happened when I ended up at a four-hour lunch with an 83-year-old man.

Another time, a friend invited me to come on a cruise with him. Both of them offered me money and an opportunity to have all my physical needs met if I would marry them.

But the thing is, the scripture says, 'What does it profit you if you gain the world and lose your soul?' If I went with them, I would be abandoning the path God has chosen for me.

Hello? It makes me understand how women and men get caught in human trafficking. It's because they're desperate. You have to understand, when you are desperate for food, or love, or shelter, or drugs, or belonging, you get caught. If you believe their promises of money and love, that's when you get caught.

Most of the time, if you're caught by human traffickers, it's because you are coming from a poor family, and something that you need is missing in your life.

Often, the need is for acceptance.

I'm always trying to fit in, but I'm coming to the point where I realize that I don't *have* to fit in, because Jesus's love is enough to fill up all of my needs.

SECOND CONVERSION

My friend's father is the founder of the homeless Rescue Mission in Martinsburg, West Virginia, so one year, I went to the Christmas Eve party there. I sat in the back row with all the homeless men from all walks of life as the pastor talked about the birth of Christ out of the Gospel of Luke.

The homeless men were singing Christmas songs with full voice, from their hearts. I sat there and thought about the churches I've sat in where three-fourths of the congregation never sings. When those men sang "Silent

Night," I cried. They sang it with the kindness and purity of love.

They all cared about each other. One kid had lime green hair, another had long stringy grey hair. When you look at them you see the people that society doesn't want around. But they know it's the kindness that matters.

All of a sudden, there was a slow-moving light in the room. That light hit each man, hovering over every one of them. Then it came and stopped in front of me. The light penetrated into my heart and told me the scripture verse, "As you do unto the least of these, you do it unto me."

Then the light spread out inside of me and scooped out my ego and other gunk, just like an ice cream scoop. What came out of me dissolved, and it flew out into the universe like little flies. Something like sparkles formed in the scoop and went inside of me, changing me. There was a kindness and a calm in me that wasn't there before. I felt totally different. Totally connected to God. It was like a deliverance, but it was a deeper feeling than when I got delivered.

The service continued, but when it was over, the light left and a sense of total kindness settled over the room.

My friends and I went from there to Waffle House, where I got a cup of hot tea. I looked out at all the people in the restaurant, and suddenly, here was the light again. It traveled through Waffle House like it was looking for something, and this time it only set on one person, a tattooed cook. He turned around, looked at me, and smiled. Between us was the same sense of kindness and calm.

Then, my phone rang, and I learned a young person had overdosed on heroin and died. The family wanted to talk to me. Would I come on Christmas Day?

On Christmas morning, I drove to the next state to talk with the family. I did not know that when I got there the doors were going to open and secrets were going to pour out. The light came in as I spoke with the family. I was the only one who could see it, but hidden things just started coming out of everyone. The family, their minister, the hostess were just spilling, and I sat there trying to give direction and perspective. I tried to show them that instead of going to the church for help, the family kept their son's heroin addiction a secret. And now the boy is dead. How many other people in the church are stuck in secret addictions? How can we help each other more?

The light's scooping changed me. When I drove down the road, the colors and views were more detailed. A message of Wayne Dyer's I had been listening to became so much clearer: Be like an ocean, so mighty, but lower than any other body of water. Everything flows into it because it is lower down. Live with less. Be simple. The light allowed me to know that it will penetrate people. The light is God. It's God's purity, the purity of love. I knew it without a doubt. It is Christ's love. An energy.

Most people are still so caught in the world. They serve God and help others, but they are caught on earth. They have resentments. That cook was tattooed up and down his neck and down both of his arms, but he was open. He was not so caught in the material world. I would venture to say he probably came off the streets and out of jail and has had it hard. Somewhere, he learned that it's kindness that matters. Others are caught in their ego, which is bigger than their kindness. It's hard to change, because once you get caught up in wanting "more, more, more," you get addicted.

All you have to do is be really open and God will use you.

Listen to your intuition. Are you willing to move with his Spirit? Are you going to be more in tune with God or are you going to stay caught in the world?

Some nights, I go downtown to where the prostitutes are

working. I talk to them, give them little sample bottles of toothpaste and things. Mostly, I'm just kind. Just letting the love of Jesus Christ come out of me and into them.

One day, I got a real compliment. One of the ladies came to Burger King just as I was getting off shift. She bought a sandwich and sat down to talk.

"Ms. Penny, the girls and me decided we want you to be our leader. You're nice to us, and you'd make sure we only get the good customers."

It's the love of Jesus Christ, coming through to them.

WHO IS PENNY KAY?

Now, I can see who I am in Christ. Now, I understand what He called me to be:

- o Pioneer
- o Woman of Faith
- o Warrior
- o Entrepreneur
- o Pure, positive-flowing energy
- o Compassionate

I understand through the physics that Christ's love is so pure it will break down any walls. I am just a broken vessel he chooses to use.

I've come to understand that I am put in locations where I am only there for a short time and then I'm gone again.

Essentially, I am a compassionate warrior; a daughter of the King.

I am my own individual person, but I take wisdom from other people, and I learn. I've had a very interesting life, and I still have lots to go yet, more learning. It's getting more exciting. I don't have worries anymore. I've let go of that. Today is today. And I really, really work at practicing kindness

131

in everything. I choose that instead of being upset with someone. It's amazing how life is changing because of it.

My job is to guide people. I can see when a person's motives or intentions are not what they claim, but I don't say anything. I just show them compassion and help them get through what they're going through. I guide them.

I don't believe there are evil people. The seven deadly sins are a Shadow. People allow the part of themselves that is influenced by greed, lust, gluttony, etc., to be bigger than the part of them that lives in the Light. I just have to show compassion so people can learn to stay in the Light.

MY TREATMENT PHILOSOPHY

I am a pioneer because I am dealing holistically with human trafficking victims. Traditional therapy is not working. Victims need to be loved and cared about. I know this first hand! I'd really like to go to Taiwan to the place where that couple works with those young kids. *The Pink Room* – a documentary about how they left everything in the US to go help kids who were sold into sex trafficking. Just sit next to them. Don't touch, don't talk. Just be there with them. It takes a kind of total patience. That's what I want to do. Many of the young trafficked girls are turning around and becoming the traffickers because the traditional methods of healing them are not working.

In recovery from human trafficking, just like in AA, we don't dwell on the past. Instead, we remember and honor the person who was there on the journey, and then we move forward.

One of my goals is to educate people about avoiding human traffickers. The people who really need to hear how not to get caught in human trafficking are not being taught. Official "programs" don't go into the gullies of West Virginia and talk to people about not letting their son or daughter be photographed.

132

Or how to protect the kids who are mentally challenged. They may not have minds that work, but they have a body that can be misused.

To avoid being trafficked, you really have to get into the Holy Spirit because you have no way of knowing if the well dressed person you're talking to is a trafficker. Go with your gut. The Holy Spirit will tell you.

I'm teaching people to stop posting pictures of their kids on Facebook, and stop putting up their location information.

The lady with me at AA has a son with autism. Two weeks ago some guy came and was talking to her son – a stranger – and was enticing him with a game. He was right there in the neighborhood. She went out and confronted him. She said, "If I hadn't have seen him, I might not have had a son today. Thank you for teaching me, because I wouldn't have said anything to him otherwise."

How many times when I spoke did the poor people come up to talk to me afterwards, only to have the higher class come and try to push them away? I didn't let that happen. The poor endure the beatings and the mistreatment of the world just to get a few crumbs. It's the poor whose children suffer so badly. That's why the poor were so close to Jesus's heart. He knew how they were treated, and he loved them.

Teaching people to follow their dreams is also close to my heart. Once, in a Bible study, I taught a family that they could follow their dreams. They sold everything, moved to Montana, bought some raw land, and started building – it was their dream. Sometimes, I send them a little money and tell them to do something crazy with it!

Those are the two prongs of my message: how to avoid trafficking and, instead, follow your dreams.

I don't need to go all over the world with this message; I just need to go out.

Lynnette, who lets me rent her camper, is the child of a rape, so she carries a weight of unworthiness. When you start helping someone, you find a web that you start unraveling. I don't want to be a counselor who sits in an office with someone for 50 minutes at a time. I want to leave a legacy. I want to be like the saying: people don't remember what you did for them or said to them, but how you made them feel.

I don't care if they never remember my name.

This is a way that God is restoring "the years that the locust has eaten." (Joel 2:25)

LIFE OUT HERE ON THE EDGE

Sometimes, it's hard, and I feel distraught because God pushes me right to the edge. I'm alone and don't have a financial safety net. Not an extra cent to my name! Sometimes I feel like I'm coming apart wondering where the next meal will come from or why things happen the way they do. But then, at that point when I can't take any more, God will literally reach down and take care of me. I'll get a call from a veteran who heard me talk at the VA a year ago and now he and his girlfriend are getting married and they have a prison ministry. He is sober, and he calls me just to say thank you for teaching him in that meeting two years ago.

That's what God does.

When I'm screaming and yelling at the very edge, he shows me how he has used me to help people. That gives me the strength to carry on. It totally does.

There is no way to put it in words for people to really understand how I live. They just don't get it. The way God works with me is one step at a time. I yell at God, but I don't complain. I thank him for everything I get. I also obey him when he tells me to do something.

If you're obedient to the Holy Spirit, your actions start planting seeds.

I did a walk. A girl in Wisconsin did a 200-mile run.

A man is driving around the US raising awareness for human trafficking. Someone else sees it and does something

134

else. God picks it up and multiplies it in a continuous ripple effect. You do what is in your spirit and it spreads.

You have to get to that point where you are content to wait until God tells you it's time. That's when it gets scary because we as humans want to *do*. But it's easy. Just wait for God.

Most people are caught. They are programmed to think they need money. They have to pay this bill and that bill, but in other parts of the world, you don't need money.

One little speck of light dispels the darkness, but one spot of dark does not put out the light. Send the world a blessing by letting God take over.

I've reached the point where I realize this all happened to me, but I have so much to do that I need to put my energy into the future, not into dwelling on the past.

I have always seen my glass as half full. That hope is so deep inside me that I know if things don't work out one way, they'll work out another.

There are people in their last days that I am going to be with. That's why I can't be tied down. There are people I need to see. The overwhelming feeling came over me as I was chopping onions at Burger King – there are people I need to see. The Holy Spirit says, "I need you to see these people so that they can do the things they need to do."

The way I live just doesn't fit with the regular world. That's the thing. That's me standing in front of the receptionist at a local church as she says, "I don't know how you live the way you do!" I'm saying, "That's right, you really *don't* know what it's like to live my life!"

Penny Kay's work to raise awareness about the issue of human trafficking in the United States and around the world is funded by generous donors like you. If you would like to host a speaking event or become a part of this work, contact:

Coffeehouse Farm
P.O. Box 669
Gerrardstown, WV 25420

Made in the USA
Columbia, SC
08 November 2018